Elemen[illegible]
Math Games

Classroom-Tested Math Activities

Math Games products available in print or eBook form.

Elementary • Middle School

Written by
Miryam Alter

Edited by
Patricia Gray

THE CRITICAL THINKING CO.™
www.CriticalThinking.com
Phone: 800-458-4849 • Fax: 541-756-1758
1991 Sherman Ave., Suite 200 • North Bend • OR 97459
ISBN 978-1-60144-932-0

Printed in the United States of America by Sheridan Books, Inc., Chelsea, MI (June 2018)

Table of Contents

About the Games

Do any of the following scenarios sound familiar?

- A class has completed a math topic and the students need to be challenged to use their new skills.
- A teacher is looking for different ways of assessing math skills, critical thinking, and understanding math concepts.
- A class needs to revisit, in a unique way, a math topic that has already been taught.
- A teacher wants activities that enable students to look for patterns.
- A teacher wants varied opportunities for students to develop and articulate their strategies for problem solving.
- A class seems unenthusiastic about their studies today, and the teacher wants to perk up their interest.
- A teacher wants an activity that is easily explained so that most of the allotted class time is spent doing the activity itself.
- A teacher-in-training needs a resource that describes activities not found in the standard text book.
- Parents want to extend math learning at home using fun ways to practice and enrich.

This book is a compilation of games for Grades 3-5 that accomplish all of the above. Each game has been classroom-tested numerous times, sparking the interest of even the most indifferent math student. Knowing how valuable classroom and preparation time is, each game has clear and concise instructions and all the reproducible master sheets necessary for playing.

Materials needed are listed at the beginning of each game description. Most of the games require only pencil, paper, and a pair of dice or a spinner. Access to a random number generator is helpful. There are many on-line sites that provide this:

http://www.mathgoodies.com/calculators/random_no_custom
http://www.randomlists.com/random-numbers

Students learn at different paces and different levels. **Variations** describe alternative ways of playing the game, either by advancing to a more challenging level or simplifying.

An intriguing question can get students to stretch their thinking. Look for this section: **Questions for Further Discovery**.

Use these games to facilitate assessment. Since students are eager to play the games, they are not reluctant to ask for help to improve their understanding of the math vocabulary or the concepts used in the game. It then becomes clear which concepts need review and which students may need that review.

Use these games as a catalyst for class discussions about students' strategies. As students articulate their strategies to their peers, their understanding of the math concept is re-enforced. Students learn to appreciate the diverse thinking of their classmates. Often, when using these games, teachers have remarked, "I didn't know that student could think so deeply about numbers!"

Use these games as an Invaluable tool to help with computational fluency. Students want to be able to use numbers and operations accurately so they can successfully play the game.

Students often just want to know "how" to do a problem and not the "why" behind what needs to be done to solve it. Not knowing the "why" prevents them from knowing when to apply the solution process to other problems. "Teachable Moments," the last chapter, describes "digging deeper" into the "why it works" of some of the math concepts taught and used in these games.

A study of the latest educational research has corroborated that there are a myriad of ways that games help children become proficient math learners. An article published by the University of Chicago, "Learning Mathematics Through Games," (2015), listed the following benefits of using games:

- Meaningful situations – for the application of mathematical skills
- Motivation – children enjoy playing
- Positive attitude – games reduce the fear of failure and error
- Increased learning – increased interaction between children and more opportunities to test intuitive ideas and problem-solving strategies
- Different levels – games allow children to operate at different levels of thinking
- Assessment – children's thinking becomes apparent through actions and decisions they make during a game

For the teacher's convenience, a chart (page 146) is provided showing which math concepts and skills are developed and practiced in each individual game. Student Activity pages are available for copying as PDFs at www.criticalthinking.com/emg.

Watch a class playing these games and you will see even the most uninterested math student sitting on the edge of his or her seat. Students want to do the computation. They want to know what the math vocabulary means. They want to create strategies. All this, because they want to play the game!

There is nothing as rewarding to a teacher as the powerful moment when a student's face lights up with the expression, "I can do math!" Enjoy these moments as your class plays these games.

Technology Tips

The Internet Random Number Generator will allow you to choose an interval of numbers from -500 to 500. Choose the interval of numbers you will be using based on the comfort level of your class. Enter that interval into the random number generator. Spinners, dice and random number generators can also be accessed online.
Here are two sites:

http://www.mathgoodies.com/calculators/random_no_custom
http://www.randomlists.com/random-numbers

About the Author

Miryam Alter has taught elementary and middle school math for the past thirty-two years. She is chairperson of the math department at Manhattan Day School, and in this capacity coaches all math teachers within the school and oversees the math curriculum, Grades 1-8.

She taught math courses to teachers for seventeen years in the Bank Street College of Education's Math Leadership Masters program.

She has given numerous math workshops for the Gruss Educational Foundation and Teaching Matters Inc. to schools in the metropolitan area. She has also presented math workshops to education majors at Stern College and Touro College.

She graduated from Brooklyn College, Phi Beta Kappa, Magna Cum Laude, with a major in mathematics. She has a Masters Degree in Computer Education from the Bank Street College of Education.

In Appreciation

Thank you to the publishing staff at The Critical Thinking Co.™ for making a dream into a reality.
Thank you to my colleagues at Manhattan Day School for all their encouragement and support, especially during our "math meetings."
Thank you to my sister, Rochelle Sherwinter, my first math teacher.
Thank you to Dr. Barbara Dubitsky, my mentor at Bank Street. I walked into her class thinking I knew what good teaching was. I walked out of her class realizing what great teaching is.

This book is dedicated to my husband, Amos, my partner in everything I do and to the inspiration of our lives, our children and grandchildren.

Helpful Math Terms

Commutative: The sum or product of two numbers does not change when the order in which two numbers are added or multiplied changes.

Composite Number: A number that has more factors than 1 and itself. All whole numbers above 1 are either composite or prime. Example: 91 is a composite number because its factors are 1; 7; 13; 91.

Computation: Finding an answer by using mathematics (addition, subtraction, multiplication, division).

Difference: The result of subtraction.

Factor: A number that divides another number with a remainder of zero. Or similarly, when numbers are multiplied together, each is a factor of the resulting product. Example: 16 ÷ 8 = 2, 8 is a factor of 16. 8 x 2 = 16, 2 and 8 are factors of 16.

Integer: A whole number.

Interval: The numbers between two specific values.

Multiple: The multiples of a number include all the numbers that result from multiplying that number by any whole number. Example: The multiples of 3 are 3; 6; 9; 12; 15; etc.

Order of Operations (PEMDAS): The rules that say which calculation comes first in an expression (Parentheses, Exponents, Multiply, Divide, Add, Subtract).

Palindrome Number: Reads the same backwards and forwards. Example: 55; 161; 1001; 61416, etc.

Perfect Square: The result of multiplying a whole number by itself. Example: 16 is a perfect square because 4 x 4 = 16.

Power (of a number): The number of times a number is multiplied by itself. It is written as a small number to the right and above the base number. Example: 83 = 8 x 8 x8; 8 is the base and 3 is the power.

Prime Number: A number that has exactly two factors: 1 and itself.

Product: The result of multiplication.

Quotient: The result of division.

Square Number: The answer after multiplying a whole number by itself. Example: 4 × 4 = 16, so 16 is a square number.

Game 1
GREATER THAN, LESS THAN

Materials

- Pencil and paper
- Pair of dice, spinner, or Internet random number generator
    - Internet sites for the random number generator
        - http://www.mathgoodies.com/calculators/random_no_custom
        - http://www.randomlists.com/random-numbers
- Overhead, white board, or Smartboard (optional)
- Student activity sheets (pages 7-12)

Learning Standards for Mathematics

- Fluency using the four operations (addition, subtraction, multiplication, division)
- Use equations to compare numerical quantities
- Generate and analyze patterns
- Perform operations with multi-digit whole numbers
- Compare fractions—equivalence and ordering
- Compare decimals by reasoning about their size
- Use symbols such as <, >, or =
- Interpret numerical expressions

– Overview –

Students practice with the concept, vocabulary, and symbols of inequalities. This game encourages students to make sense of quantities and their relationships. Students must reflect not only on the quantities themselves, but also on the outcome of a particular mathematical operation. Estimation and accurate computation of sums and differences are necessary for maintaining the inequality. Students are required to plan ahead and strategize about where to place a number. This activity can be played on different levels depending on the operations and intervals of the numbers that are used.

– The Game –

Use Student Activity Sheet (page 7). The object of the activity is to keep the sum of the numbers on the left side of the equation greater than the sum of the numbers on the right side of the equation.

Draw the diagram on page 2 on an overhead, whiteboard, or Smartboard. Then announce the interval from which the numbers will be chosen during the activity. A number is randomly chosen using either a die, several pairs of dice, spinner, or Internet random number generator. The student places the number obtained in one of the blank spots on her/his student activity sheet. Once it is written in a space, it cannot be changed. This process is repeated four times. The object is to keep the sum of the numbers on the left side of the equation greater than the sum of the numbers on right side of the equation.

Example: Use the generated numbers **3**, **2**, **4**, **5**.

The first number generated is a **3**. The student places the 3 in one of the blanks.

__________ + __________ > __________ + ____3____

The second number generated is a **2**.

__________ + __________ > ____2____ + ____3____

The third number generated is a **4**.

____4____ + __________ > ____2____ + ____3____

The fourth number generated is a **5**.

____4____ + ____5____ > ____2____ + ____3____

9 > 5! Yes, the inequality was maintained!

Asking a student how she/he is sure the inequality was maintained, you might think she/he summed both sides and realized that 9 > 5. For example, a student might say, "I know 5 is greater than 2 and 4 is greater than 3, so I know the left side is greater than the right side." That's how you want students to think about numbers!

Teachers are forever re-explaining the greater than/less than symbol (9 **>** 5, 5 **<** 9) and trying to invent ways for students to remember which side of the equation represents the greater number. After playing this game, students don't forget!

– Game Variations –

a. **Smallest Difference:** Use the Student Activity Sheet (page 8). The object is to get the left side of the inequality to be greater than the right side of the inequality, but with the smallest difference possible.

Example: Use the generated numbers **3, 2, 4, 5**.

What is the smallest difference possible?

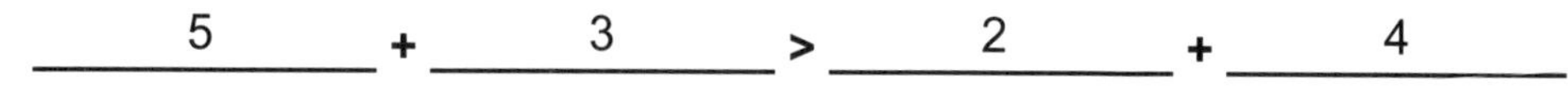

8 > 6, the difference is **2**!

b. **Different Operations:** Use the Student Activity Sheet (page 9). The object is to use subtraction, multiplication, or division instead of addition to maintain the inequality.

Example: Use the generated numbers **2, 3, 4, 5**.

Subtraction

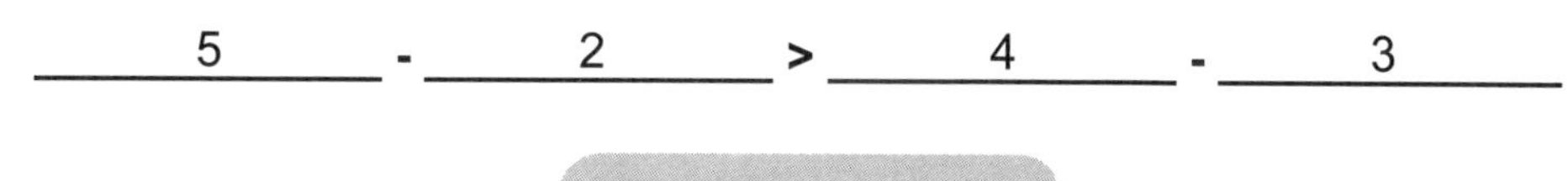

3 > 1 You did it!

Multiplication

5 x 3 > 2 x 4

15 > 8 You did it!

Division or Fractions

5 ÷ 3 > 2 ÷ 4

$\mathbf{\frac{5}{3} > \frac{2}{4}}$ You did it!

c. **Use the Four Operations to Change the Numbers:** Use the Student Activity Sheet (page 10). The object is to use the sum, difference, product, or quotient of the numbers generated. Choose only one operation per round.

Example*:* The operation for this round is multiplication. The first numbers generated are **5** and **4** product is 20.

________ + ___20___ > ________ + ________

The second numbers generated are **6** and **4**, product is **24**.

___24___ + ___20___ > ________ + ________

The third numbers generated are **6** and **5**, product is **30**.

___24___ + ___20___ > ___30___ + ________

Hoping for low numbers!

The fourth numbers generated are **6** and **6**, product is **36**.

___24___ + ___20___ > ___30___ + ___36___

44 is <u>not</u> greater than **66**. Unfortunately, this did not maintain the inequality!

Question for Further Discovery

What combination would have maintained the inequality?

20 + 36 > 24 + 30

d. **Comparing Decimals:** Use the Student Activity Sheet (page 11). This is using a decimal point to each side of the inequality sign.

. ______ ______ > . ______ ______

Example: The first number generated is **5**.

. ______ ___5___ > . ______ ______

The second number generated is **4**.

. ______ ___5___ > . ______ ___4___

The third number generated is **3**.

. ____ __5__ > . __3__ __4__

Hoping for a number greater than 3.

The fourth number generated is **2**.

. __2__ __5__ > . __3__ __4__

Unfortunately, **.25 < .34**. The inequality is not maintained.

e. **Comparing Fractions and Decimals:** Use the Student Activity Sheet (page 12). The number on the right is a decimal with two decimal places. The number on the left may be an integer or fraction.

____ ÷ ____ > . ____ ____

Example: The first number generated is **5**.

____ ÷ ____ > . ____ __5__

The second number generated is **2**.

__2__ ÷ ____ > . ____ __5__

The third number generated is **3**.

__2__ ÷ __3__ > . ____ __5__

The fourth number generated is **4**.

__2__ ÷ __3__ > . __4__ __5__

Yes! $\frac{2}{3}$ **> .45**

Reverse the numbers for a different board.

. ____ ____ > ____ ÷ ____

Questions for Further Discovery

1 What strategies did you use? For instance, "if a 1 comes up, I put it in the denominator on the left." Will this always work? What about the situation below?

It is helpful to realize that the blanks represent the numerator and denominator of a fraction.

numerator ÷ denominator > numerator ÷ denominator

Try to place numbers on the right side so that the division results in a proper fraction. The numerator should be less than the denominator on that side. The reverse is true of the left side. Try to place the numbers so that the division results in a number greater than 1, the numerator is greater than the denominator.

3 ÷ 1 > 6 ÷ 2

That doesn't work. The left side equal the right side.

2 What about the situation below if you are using a 10-sided die?

4 ÷ 1 > 9 ÷ 2

Using the strategies above, create proper fractions and keep the numbers closest together on one side.

3 Strategies are definitely helpful. But sometimes there are exceptions! Can you think of situations where the strategy you used will not work? Will it work if you are trying to get the smallest difference?

That works!

Student Activity Sheet

Greater Than, Less Than

(Addition)

__________ + __________ > __________ + __________

__________ + __________ > __________ + __________

__________ + __________ > __________ + __________

__________ + __________ > __________ + __________

Student Activity Sheet

Greater Than, Less Than

(Variation: a. Smallest Difference)

______________ + ______________ > ______________ + ______________

______________ + ______________ > ______________ + ______________

______________ + ______________ > ______________ + ______________

______________ + ______________ > ______________ + ______________

Student Activity Sheet

Greater Than, Less Than

(Variation: b. Different Operations)

_______________ + _______________ > _______________ + _______________

_______________ - _______________ > _______________ - _______________

_______________ x _______________ > _______________ x _______________

_______________ ÷ _______________ > _______________ ÷ _______________

Student Activity Sheet

Greater Than, Less Than

(Variation: c. Using the Four Operations to Change the Numbers)

____________ + ____________ > ____________ + ____________

____________ - ____________ > ____________ - ____________

____________ x ____________ > ____________ x ____________

____________ ÷ ____________ > ____________ ÷ ____________

Student Activity Sheet

Greater Than, Less Than

(Variation: d. Comparing Decimals)

. ________ ________ > . ________ ________

. ________ ________ > . ________ ________

. ________ ________ > . ________ ________

. ________ ________ > . ________ ________

Student Activity Sheet

Greater Than, Less Than

(Variation: e. Comparing Fractions and Decimals)

. ____________ ____________ > ____________ ÷ ____________

. ____________ ____________ > ____________ ÷ ____________

. ____________ ____________ > ____________ ÷ ____________

. ____________ ____________ > ____________ ÷ ____________

Game 2
STAND UP AND BE COUNTED!

Materials

- Pencil and paper
- **Stand Up and Be Counted** cards (pages 16-18)
- Index cards

Learning Standards for Mathematics

- Fluency using the four operations
- Gain familiarity with factors and multiples
- Generate a number pattern that follows a certain rule
- Interpret numerical expressions
- Analyze relationships between numbers
- Perform operations with multi-digit whole numbers

– Overview –

Vocabulary is an important part of math fluency and precision. Math vocabulary words should be introduced and used frequently when referring to the corresponding math concepts they describe. Students need to know the meaning of many math vocabulary words and how to apply that knowledge to the numbers they have chosen. Students feel they are on their way to becoming mathematicians when they know the vocabulary and symbols of mathematics! This activity helps students understand, practice, and apply their math vocabulary.

– The Game –

Ask each student to randomly choose and write down ten numbers between 1 and 100. Change the interval of numbers based on the level and fluency of the class. Cut out the appropriate class level **Stand Up and Be Counted** cards. On each card is a statement describing a category of numbers. Cards can be mixed and matched between different sets. (Level B and C cards are to used in conjunction with Level A cards and not independently.) Possible cards for each level are given below and on the next page.

Possible Level A Cards

- Two-digit number
- Multiple of 4
- Odd number
- Multiple of 2 and 3
- Odd number that is a multiple of 7
- Number in 5s times table, but not in 4s times table
- 5 in the ones' position
- Even number
- Factor of 24
- Number whose tens digit is less than 8
- Greater than 60, but less than 75
- Multiple of 9

Level B Cards

- Prime number
- Composite number
- Multiple of 6
- Multiple of 7
- Factor of 64
- Palindrome number
- Factor of 56
- Less than 25 that is a factor of 50.
- Greater than 75 that is a multiple of 12
- Within interval $29 < x < 63$
- Factor of 45 and 81
- Multiple of 2, 3, 4

Level C Cards

- Prime number
- Composite number
- Perfect square
- Factor of 99
- Power of 2
- Multiple of 2, 3, and 7
- Greater than 50 that is a palindrome
- Factor of 18, 54, and 72
- Multiple of 5, but not a multiple of 15
- Factor of 42, but not of 56
- Within interval $43 < x < 73$
- Third of the number is a prime number

Read a descriptive statement from one of the cards to the class. If the descriptive statement describes a number on the student's list, she/he circles that number. If more than one number on the list is described, only one number may be circled.

Example: The student's numbers are 10, 5, 7, 14, 22, 9, 1, 54, 17, and 88. The descriptive statement on the card is: **Two-digit number**. The student may circle only one of the following from his list: 10, 14, 22, 54, 17, or 88.

After reading a descriptive statement card, attach it to a board. When using a Smartboard, use the shade option to reveal only the descriptive statements you have read.

After ten descriptive statement cards are read, a student who has circled all her/his numbers stands and reads the numbers. As the student reads each of the numbers, she/he indicates which descriptive statement describes that number.

If no student has circled all of her/his numbers after the ten descriptive statements are read, either read new statements or use the same statements again, randomly choosing one at a time. A student who has circled all her/his numbers, immediately stands after the last number has been circled and reads the numbers. Again, as the student reads each of the numbers, she/he indicates which descriptive statement describes that number.

– Teaching Management Tip –

It is sometimes difficult to remember which descriptive statement applies to which number. For instance, you have the numbers 9, 12, and 15. Which did you use as an odd number, which did you use as a multiple of 3, and which did you use as a number less than 20? Many students can come up with a helpful method. Each student writes a little hint about the descriptive category next to the circled number. Numbering the descriptive statements is also helpful. The student then puts the number of the descriptive statement next to the circled number on her/his list.

– Game Variations –

a. Ask each student to write a descriptive statement on an index card. Collect the cards. Ask the students to choose ten numbers from the appropriate interval. Randomly choose ten of the collected cards as the first ten descriptive statements to be read. Call on ten students, one at a time, to read the descriptive statement from their cards. Make sure to display the descriptive statements after each one is read.

b. Ask each student to write down a descriptive statement on an index card and choose five numbers that are described in the descriptive statement. Call on a student to write her/his numbers on the whiteboard or Smartboard. Ask the class to guess the descriptive statement on the student's card. Are there other descriptive statements that could describe the numbers the student chose?

Questions for Further Discovery

Use the interval **1-100.**

1. What is a descriptive statement that would describe at least twenty numbers?

   Example: Prime Numbers, Odd Numbers, Even Numbers

2. What is a descriptive statement that would describe at most ten numbers?

   Example: Numbers ending in 0. A number less than 25, but greater than or equal to 15.

3. What is a descriptive number that will describe exactly nineteen numbers?

   Example: A group of numbers containing a particular number.
   (2, 12, 120, 21, 22, 23, 24, 25, 26, 27, 28, 29, 32, 42, 52, 62, 72, 82, 92)
   A number greater than 40 but less than or equal to 59.

4. What is a descriptive statement that would describe only one number in each group of tens?

   Example: A number whose sum of digits equals 9. A number whose one's digit is 3.

5. What is a descriptive statement that would describe only one number?

   Example: A number larger than 5 but smaller than 7 (6). A prime number whose digits add up to 13 (67).

Level A Cards
STAND UP AND BE COUNTED!

A1 **Two-digit number**	A7 **5 in the ones position**
A2 **Multiple of 4**	A8 **Even number**
A3 **Odd number**	A9 **Factor of 24**
A4 **Multiple of 2 and 3**	A10 **Tens digit is less than 8**
A5 **Odd number that is a multiple of 7**	A11 **Greater than 60, but less than 75**
A6 **In 5s times table, but not in 4s times table**	A12 **Multiple of 9**

Level B Cards
STAND UP AND BE COUNTED!

B1 **Prime number**	B7 **Factor of 56**
B2 **Composite number**	B8 **Less than 25 that is a factor of 50**
B3 **Multiple of 6**	B9 **Greater than 75 that is a multiple of 12**
B4 **Multiple of 7**	B10 **Within interval $29 < x < 63$**
B5 **Factor of 64**	B11 **Factor of 45 and 81**
B6 **Palindrome number**	B12 **A multiple of 2, 3, 4**

Level C Cards
STAND UP AND BE COUNTED!

C1 **Prime Number**	C7 **Greater than 50 that is a palindrome**
C2 **Composite Number**	C8 **Factor of 18, 54, 72**
C3 **Perfect square**	C9 **Multiple of 5, but not a multiple of 15**
C4 **Factor of 99**	C10 **Factor of 42, but not a factor of 56**
C5 **Power of 2**	C11 **Within the interval** $43 < x < 73$
C6 **Multiple of 2, 3, 7**	C12 **A third of the number is a prime number**

Game 3
CLAP YOUR HANDS! STOMP YOUR FEET!

Materials
- Index cards with one number from 2 to 15 on each card
- Musical Instruments (optional)
- Smartboard (optional)
- Internet counter (free on Internet)
- Metronome

Learning Standards in Mathematics
- Gain familiarity with the concept of factors and multiples
- Practice with factors and multiples to gain fluency

– Overview –

This activity is a delightful way to combine fluency with multiples and music. It also makes for a great video!

– The Game –

Each student (or group) gets a card with a number from the interval 2 through 15. Count at a steady beat to 100, using an Internet number counter, Smartboard counter, or counting orally. Every time the counter reaches a multiple of the number on the card received, the student (or group) claps hands or stomps feet.

Distribute musical instruments such as cymbals, drums, or triangles and have the students use them when the counter reaches a multiple of the number on their cards. You'll be making beautiful music!

– Game Variation –

Hand a student a card so no one in the class sees the number she/he is receiving and have her/him stand. Start the counting, but this time start at the number 20 or greater. The student proceeds to clap when she/he recognizes a multiple of the number on her/his card. Have the class guess what number is on the student's card.

Questions for Further Discovery

Write the numbers distributed to the class on the board.

1 Which of these numbers will get the most claps? Which the least?

Answers will vary.

2 At what number will more than one group clap?

Answers will vary.

3 At what number will no group clap?

Answers will vary.

Game 4
CAN YOU MAKE.....?

Materials

- Pencil and paper
- Index cards
- Timer
- Overhead, whiteboard, or Smartboard (optional)

Learning Standards for Mathematics

- Fluency using the four operations
- Generate and analyze patterns
- Perform operations with multi-digit whole numbers
- Interpret numerical expressions

– Overview –

Students use number sense, operational skills, and strategies to compute a target number from five randomly chosen numbers. Operational fluency and precision is an asset in this activity.

– The Game –

Distribute six index cards to each student. Each student randomly picks five numbers from 1 to 25 (or from any appropriate interval for the class level) and writes down each number on a separate card. The sixth card is for keeping score. Choose any number from 1 to 50 (or from any interval that is appropriate for your class level) and write it on the board. To involve the students in choosing the number, pick any student, ask the number of the day of her/his birthday, and use that number.

Students have an allotted time (about 1 to 1.5 minutes) to use at least two numbers from their cards and any operation (addition, subtraction, multiplication, and division) to help compute the number on the board. A student must use at least two numbers from her/his cards to compute the number. The same number may not be used twice in any one computation.

As soon as a student has an answer, they raise their hand. When the allotted time is up, students with raised hands will be called on to explain their answers. A correct answer gains one point.

Students should have an index card on which to keep track of their score. This is a good time to use tallying. As students accumulate their scores, explain that keeping score in groups of 5 is so much easier when computing the final score. Look at the difference for a score of 12: |||||||||||| or 𝍸 𝍸 ||.

Example:

The numbers on my cards are 5, 10, 11, 13, 7

The number on the board is 25.

Possible answer: 13 + 7 + 10 - 5 = 25

The amazing outcomes – Every number on the board will have at least one solution within the class!

Questions for Further Discovery

1. Based on the interval chosen for the cards, for example 1 to 25, what is the highest target number you could compute?

   25 x 24 x 23 x 22 = 303,600.

2. If the number cards only have odd numbers, what computations must you do to get an even result?

   Some suggestions might be:
   Add an even amount of your odd numbers
   Subtract two odd numbers.

3. If the number cards only have even numbers, is it possible to get an odd result?

   Yes, if you use division.
   Even + Even = Even
   Even - Even = Even
   Even × Even = Even
   Even ÷ Even = odd or even depending on the numbers.
   12 ÷ 6 = 2   12 ÷ 4 = 3
   See "Teachable Moments" (page 133) for further study of odd and even numbers.

Game 5
MATH IN A CIRCLE

Materials
- **Math in a Circle** cards (pages 25-28)
- Overhead, whiteboard, or Smartboard (optional)

Learning Standards for Mathematics
- Fluency using the four operations
- Generate and analyze patterns
- Perform operations with multi-digit whole numbers
- Interpret numerical expressions
- Use math vocabulary to indicate the necessary mathematical operation

– Overview –

Students use operational fluency and precision to compute a result by following the operational instructions on a distributed card. It is a great opportunity to review and practice essential math vocabulary.

– The Game –

This activity works best with groups of ten sitting in a circle. Each student is given a card with one of the following instructions on it.

1. Double the number.
2. Triple the number.
3. Divide by 6.
4. Increase by 11.
5. Decrease by 4.
6. Multiply by 3.
7. Decrease by 7.
8. Multiply by 2.
9. Divide by 10.
10. Multiply by 3.

Distribute the **Math in a Circle** cards (page 25) in numerical order and supply the starting number. Using the starting number, the first student follows the instructions on the card and announces the result. The next student continues. Using the result of the student that came before her/him, the student follows the instructions on her/his own card.

Example: Starting number is **2**.

Card Instructions	**Student Announces**
Double the number.	The result is 4.
Triple the number.	The result is 12.
Divide by 6.	The result is 2.
Increase by 11.	The result is 13.
Decrease by 4.	The result is 9.
Multiply by 3.	The result is 27.
Decrease by 7.	The result is 20.
Multiply by 2.	The result is 40.
Divide by 10.	The result is 4.
Multiply by 3.	The final result is 12!

If the last student announces a result of twelve, then every student along the way computed correctly! If not, try again! It is very effective to have the final result on a sheet of paper, small lap-sized white board, or hiding on the Smartboard. Display the final answer given by the student without saying whether it is correct.

If you choose a different starting number, the algorithm for the final result is **$1.8x + 8.4$**, where *x* represents the starting number. In order to get an integer result, choose a starting number that has a 2 or a 7 in the ones' digit.

– Game Variations –

a. Fractions or Decimals (Page 26)

Choose a starting number and give each student a card with instructions. Using the starting number, the first student follows the instructions on the card and announces the result. The next student continues. Using the result of the student that came before her/him, the student follows the instructions on her/his own card.

Example: Starting number is ½ or **.5**

Card Instructions	Student Announces
1. Double the number.	The result is 1.
2. Increase by ¼ or .25.	The result is 1 ¼ or 1.25.
3. Triple the number.	The result is 3 ¾ or 3.75.
4. Increase by ¾ or .75.	The result is 4½ or 4.50.
5. Triple the number.	The result is 13 ½ or 13.50.
6. Divide by 2.	The result is 6 ¾ or 6.75.
7. Add 3 ½ or 3.5.	The result is 10 ¼ or 10.25.
8. Subtract 6 ½ or 6.50.	The result is 3 ¾ or 3.75.
9. Divide by 3.	The result is 1 ¼ or 1.25.
10. Double the number.	The final result is 2 ½ or 2.50!

If you choose a different starting number, the final result algorithm is **$6x - .50$**, where *x* represents the starting number.

b. Larger Numbers or Two-Step Operations (Page 27)

Choose a starting number and give each student a card with instructions. Using the starting number, the first student follows the instructions on the card and announces the result. The next student continues. Using the result of the student that came before her/him, the student follows the instructions on her/his own card.

Example: Starting number is **10**.

Card Instructions	Student Announces
1. Square the number.	The result is 100.
2. Multiply by 8 and subtract 6	The result is 794.
3. Divide by 2 and add 7.	The result is 404.
4. Triple the number and add 4^2.	The result is 1,228.
5. Divide by 2 and subtract 10.	The result is 604.
6. Add 11 and divide by 3.	The result is 205.
7. Multiply by 9 and subtract 6.	The result is 1,839.
8. Divide by 3.	The result is 613.
9. Subtract 13 and multiply by 6.	The result is 3,600.
10. Take the square root of the number.	The final result is 60!

If you choose a different starting number, the final result algorithm is **$6x$**, where *x* represents the starting number.

Questions for Further Discovery

1. How does the final result compare to the starting number?

   The final result is always 6 times the starting number.

2. If we know the starting number, can we predict the final result?

   Yes.

c. **Reverse Directions:** (Page 28)

Choose a starting number and give each student a card with instructions. The student performs the operation or series of operations that are shown on the card to the starting number. She/he then announces the result of performing the instructions on the card using the starting number, without revealing what the instructions were. The other students in the class must now guess what those instructions were. Go around the circle until each student has a turn. The instructions on the card are always performed on the starting number.

Example: Starting number is **12**.

Card Instructions	Student Announces
Divide by 4.	The result is 3.
Divide by 2 and subtract 1.	The result is 5.
Square the number.	The result is 144.
Divide by 2 and square the quotient.	The result is 36.
Divide by 12.	The result is 1.
Increase by 7.	The result is 19.
Double the number and decrease by 2.	The result is 22.
Multiply the number by 4 and add 2.	The result is 50.
Subtract 3 and square the difference.	The result is 81.
Add 13 and multiply the sum by 3.	The result is 75.

Question for Further Discovery

What different instructions would result in the new number other than those on the card? It is fun and challenging to see if the students can correctly guess the instructions on the card.

Example: "Divide by 4" with "the result is 3." Could be replaced by "Take a quarter of the number."

"Multiply the number by 4 and add 2." with "The result is 50." could be replaced with "Triple the number and add 14."

Game Cards

1 Double the number

6 Multiply by 3

2 Triple the number

7 Decrease by 7

3 Divide by 6

8 Multiply by 2

4 Increase by 11

9 Divide by 10

5 Decrease by 4

10 Multiply by 3

Variation: a. Fractions or Decimals Cards

1

Double the number

2

Increase by ¼ or .25

3

Triple the number

4

Increase by ¾ or .75

5

Triple the number

6

Divide by 2

7

Add 3½ or 3.5

8

Subtract 6½ or 6.50

9

Divide by 3

10

Double the number

Variation: b. Larger Numbers or Two-Step Operations

1 Square the number

6 Add 11 and divide by 3

2 Multiply by 8 and subtract 6

7 Multiply by 9 and subtract 6

3 Divide by 2 and add 7

8 Divide by 3

4 Triple the number and add 4^2

9 Subtract 13 and multiply by 6

5 Divide by 2 and Subtract 10

10 Take the square root of the number

Variation: c. Reverse Direction Cards

1 Divide by 4

6 Increase by 7

2 Divide by 2 and subtract 1

7 Double the number and decrease by 2

3 Square the number

8 Multiply by 4 and add 2

4 Divide by 2 and square the quotient

9 Subtract 3 and square the difference

5 Divide by 12

10 Add 13 and multiply the sum by 3

Game 6
FILL THE GRID!

Materials

- **Fill the Grid** student activity sheet (page 32)
- **Target Number and Choices** sheet (page 33)
- Index cards with numbers 0-50

Learning Standards for Mathematics

- Fluency using the four operations
- Generate and analyze patterns
- Perform operations with multi-digit whole numbers

– Overview –

Students use number sense and the order of operations (PEMDAS) to fill a 5x5 grid with the correct numerical calculations. This activity emphasizes operational fluency and precision. Following the directions to fill the grid properly is challenging.

– The Game –

Each student receives a 5x5 grid. Call out or display on a board a target number, randomly chosen from cards labeled 0 through 50. The student then chooses three numbers from 1 to 9 so that by either multiplying or dividing two of the numbers, and then adding or subtracting the third number, the result will be the target number.

Example: Target number is **13**. Possible choices: (3 x 4) + 1

Using those numbers, the student places the numbers consecutively on the grid, either horizontally, vertically, or diagonally. The numbers do not have to be in the order of the operations.

	3	4	1	

		4		
	1			
3				

		4		
			3	
				1

Call out another target number and the student must choose, in the same manner described previously, three numbers to get the result of the current target number. This time however, she/he must use one of the numbers already in the grid to help her/him get to the target number. Once a number is placed on the grid, it may not be changed. The same number may be used as many times as necessary.

Example: The second target number is **26**. Using the 4 from the grid, 4 x 5 + 6 is a possible answer. The student now enters the numbers 5 and 6 into the grid. Remember the numbers can only be placed horizontally, vertically, or diagonally.

	3	4	1	
		5		
		6		

	3	4	1	
	5			
6				

	3	4	1	
			5	
				6

The game continues until 20 target numbers have been called. See how close students come to filling the entire grid.

For each target number, the student must also fill in the chart below. Use ( ) to show order of operations when necessary.

Target Number	Choices
13	3 x 4 + 1
26	4 x 5 + 6

Example:

5	7	2	8	8
4	4	6	2	3
2	1	5	7	1
2	3	1	2	2
3	8	7	6	9

Target Number	Choices
1	3 ÷ 1 - 2
12	7 x 2 - 2
25	5 x 4+5
32	6 x 5 + 2
49	(8 ÷ 1) x 7
22	5 x 4 + 2
15	6 x 2 + 3
8	2 x 8 - 8
13	2 x 5 + 3
40	7 x 6 - 2
50	8 x 7 - 6
16	7 x 2 + 2
7	4 ÷ 4 + 6
18	4 x 5 - 2
10	4 x 4 - 6
26	4 x 6 + 2
44	6 x 7 + 2
31	6 x 5 + 1
6	4 x 2 - 2
5	3 ÷ 1 + 2
0	2 x 2 - 4
11	2 ÷ 1 + 9

– Game Variation –

Distribute a successfully completed grid to the class and a list of the target numbers. Using this information, ask the students to find the choices that were made to get each target number.

Questions for Further Discovery

1. What is the largest number that can be computed using three numbers from the interval 1-9, multiplying or dividing two of the numbers, and then adding or subtracting the third number?

   9 x 8 + 7 = 79

2. Can all numbers up to the number you calculated in the above question be computed using these rules?

   The amazing answer is YES!
   1 = 7 x 1 - 6   11 = 5 x 2 + 1   21 = 5 x 4 + 1   31 = 9 x 4 - 5 ...

Student Activity Sheet
Fill the Grid!

Student Activity Sheet

Target Number	Choices

Game 7
I KNOW MY PLACE

Materials
- Pencil and paper
- Random number generator, spinner, die (optional)
  - Internet sites for the random number generator
    - http://www.mathgoodies.com/calculators/random_no_custom
    - http://www.randomlists.com/random-numbers

Learning Standards for Mathematics
- Understanding of place value and comparing quantities

– Overview –

I Know My Place encourages students to think about place value and relative quantities.

– The Game –

This activity is a whole class activity. The object of the activity is to get the largest (or smallest) number using the random numbers obtained from a random die, spinner, or number generator with digits 0-9.

Each student makes the following diagram of blank spaces:

_____ _____ _____ _____ _____

Randomly generate a number from 0 to 9. As each number is generated, the student places it in one of the blanks. This number is now locked in that place. After generating five numbers, the students discuss who created the largest (or smallest) number. Watch the excitement as the class reaches the last few blanks!

The first number generated is 5.

_____ 5 _____ _____ _____

The next 2 numbers are 8 and 2 in that order.

8 5 _____ _____ 2

The next 2 numbers generated were 1 and 9 in that order.

8 5 9 1 2

While this is a large number, the largest number was

9 8 5 2 1

– Game Variations –

a. Add more blanks to get more place values.

b. Place a decimal point in the number.

_______ _______ _______ _______ • _______ _______ _______

c. After each round, have the students order all the numbers they created.

Question for Further Discovery

Using the digits that we obtained randomly, what is the largest (or smallest) number that could have been created?

Answers will vary.

Game 8
TOP TEN WITH A TWIST!

Materials
- Deck of playing cards

Learning Standards for Mathematics
- Increase speed and fluency with sums, differences, or products of numbers

– Overview –

Top Ten with a Twist is an engaging card game that is easy to explain. Students must reflect not only on the quantities themselves, but also on the outcome of a particular mathematical operation.

– The Game –

This is a card game for 2 players. Shuffle the deck. The whole deck of cards is distributed, face down, between the players. Players reveal their top card face up, at the same time. The player with the greater number takes the revealed cards and adds them to the bottom of her/his deck.

If the revealed cards have the same value, or if the sum of two of the revealed cards is 10, it's time for the *Twist*. Each player puts 3 cards, face down, and then a fourth card, face up. The player with the greater number takes all cards and adds them to the bottom of her/his deck. Keep playing until someone wins all the cards. (Remember: Ace = 1, Jack = 11, Queen = 12, King = 13)

– Game Variations –

a. Choose a different number or numbers for the sum that causes a *Twist*.

b. Subtract the numbers on the revealed cards and choose a number for the difference that causes a *Twist*.

c. Combine *a* and *b* so that students must be adding and subtracting as they play.

d. Multiply the numbers on the revealed cards. Instead of choosing one number that causes a *Twist*, choose an interval.

Example: If the product of the numbers on the cards is greater than or equal to 25, there is a *Twist*.

Game 9
LET'S SUM UP: ODD or EVEN?

Materials

- Pencil and paper
- Dice
- **Let's Sum Up** activity sheet (page 38)

Learning Standards for Mathematics

- Fluency using the four operations
- Generate and analyze patterns

– Overview –

Students must constantly be thinking ahead as she/he calculates the results of a computation using the numbers rolled on a pair of dice. She/he asks "How can an odd or an even total sum be guaranteed at the end of five rolls of the dice and still get the largest total sum?"

– The Game –

Each round consists of rolling a pair of dice five times. Each time the dice are rolled, each player subtracts, adds, multiplies, or divides the numbers on the dice. Keep adding the results from each throw. Decide before the round starts if the winning total sum will be even or odd. The student with the largest even (or odd) total sum at the end of five throws is the winner. The student must keep two things in mind—even (or odd) and largest total sum at the end of five throws.

For each throw, fill in the **Let's Sum Up** student activity sheet (page 39).

Example:

Highest Even

Numbers on Each Throw of the Dice	Result
3, 5	3 + 5 = 8

If you play as a whole class, each player uses the numbers from the same throw. If you play in small groups or partners, each player can throw for herself/himself, and only that student can use those numbers.

Examples:

The winner is the student with the highest total even sum.

First throw: 3 and 5 — 3 + 5 = 8
Second throw: 4 and 5 — 4 x 5 = 20
Third throw: 1 and 1 — 1 + 1 = 2
Fourth throw: 3 and 4 — 3 x 4 = 12
Fifth throw: 2 and 2 — 2 x 2 or 2 + 2 = 4

Total sum: 8 + 20 + 2 + 12 + 4 = 46

Is this the highest sum possible? Let's look at this possibility: Remember only the total sum has to be even!

First throw: 3 and 5	3 x 5 = 15
Second throw: 4 and 5	4 x 5 = 20
Third throw ; 1 and 1	1 ÷ 1 = 1
Fourth throw: 3 and 4	3 x 4 = 12
Fifth throw: 2 and 2	2 x 2 or 2 + 2 = 4
	Total sum: 15 + 20 + 1 + 12 + 4 = 52!

What if the winner must have the highest odd total sum?

First throw: 3 and 5	3 x 5 = 15
Second throw: 4 and 5	4 + 5 = 9
Third throw; 1 and 1	1 x 1 or 1 ÷ 1 = 1
Fourth Throw: 3 and 4	3 + 4 = 7
Fifth throw: 2 and 2	2 ÷ 2 = 1
	Total sum: 15 + 9 + 1 + 7 + 1 = 33

Is this the highest sum possible? Let's look at this possibility: Remember only the total sum has to be odd!

First throw: 3 and 5	3 x 5 = 15
Second throw: 4 and 5	4 x 5 = 20
Third throw; 1 and 1	1 x 1 or 1 ÷ 1 = 1
Fourth Throw: 3 and 4	3 x 4 = 12
Fifth throw: 2 and 2	2 ÷ 2 = 1
	Total sum: 15 + 20 + 1 + 12 + 1 = 49

– Game Variations –

The winner of the round is the student who has the lowest even (or odd) total sum.

Lowest Total Even Sum

First throw: 3 and 5	5 - 3 = 2
Second throw: 4 and 5	5 - 4 = 1
Third throw: 1 and 1	1 - 1 = 0
Fourth throw: 3 and 4	4 - 3 = 1
Fifth throw: 2 and 2	2 - 2 = 0
	Total sum: 2 + 1 + 0 +1 + 0 = 4

Question for Further Discovery

What strategies did you use to ensure an odd or even total sum?

Answers will vary.

Student Activity Sheet
Let's Sum Up

Highest Total Even Sum

Numbers on Each Throw of the Dice	Result
1.	
2.	
3.	
4.	
5.	
Total	

Highest Total Odd Sum

Numbers on Each Throw of the Dice	Result
1.	
2.	
3.	
4.	
5.	
Total	

Game 10
MULTI-MATH BINGO

Materials

- Bingo boards (pages 41-58)
- Chips or markers

Learning Standards for Mathematics

- Fluency using the four operations
- Interpret numerical expressions symbols and verbal statements
- Operations with fractions
- Understand the decimal equivalent of a fraction

– Overview –

This is the traditional game of Bingo with a major difference. The answers on the Bingo board must first be calculated from the math expression provided by the teacher (page 41-58). There are nine Bingo boards for lots of operational practice.

– 9 Bingo Games –

- Positive Integer
- Equivalent Fractions
- Mixed Number/Integer to Improper Fraction
- Improper Fraction to Mixed Number/Integer
- Mixed Number/Improper Fraction/Proper Fraction
- Decimal to Fraction
- Fraction to Decimal
- Arabic Numerals to Roman Numerals
- Roman Numerals to Arabic Numerals

– The Game –

Give each student a Bingo board with the possible answers. Each student chooses 24 out of the 25 possible answers and writes one in each of the boxes. The student automatically gets the Free box. Write on the board and/or say orally one of the given math expressions (example: **5 x 5 + 1**). After the student has done the actual computation, she/he places a chip in the box on the Bingo board that is the result of the computation (in this case, **26**). If chips are not available, the student may just cross out the right answer. Whoever gets 5 in a row, horizontally, vertically, or diagonally, is the winner.

The student who wins must also be able to identify the math expression that resulted in the answer on the grid.

Directions: Answers are positive integers. Randomly place each possible answer below on the grid after the teacher gives the math expression for each possible answer. If you win, identify the math expressions that resulted in the answers on the grid.

Positive Integer Bingo

		FREE		

Possible Answers

9	7	12	24	16
72	90	45	21	17
8	26	30	52	70
15	22	43	37	100
50	63	29	75	13

Positive Integer Bingo

Math Expressions (called out by teacher)	Positive Integer Answers
Multiple of 3 less than 10, but greater than 7	9
15 – 8	7
3 x 4	12
14 + 10	24
2 x 10 – 4	16
5 x 5 + 1	26
8 x 10 – 8	72
100 – 5 x 2	90
9 x 5	45
6 x 4 – 3	21
3 less than twice ten	17
5 x 3 – 7	8
Multiple of 3 and 5 that is less than 20	15
Number is the same when the digits are reversed	22
9 x 5 – 2	43
Tens' digit is four less than the ones' digit	37
10 times itself (or ten squared)	100
Tens' digit is 5 times the ones' digit plus 3	30
Half of 100	50
Tens' digit is twice the ones' digit	63
Number is one less than a multiple of 10	29
3 quarters equals _____ cents	75
Odd number less than 15, but greater than 12	13
Two less than the product of 9 and 6	52
Multiple of 10 whose tens' digit is the sum of 3 and 4	70

Directions: Answers are all in reduced form. Randomly place each possible answer below on the grid after the teacher gives an equivalent fraction for each possible answer. If you win, identify the equivalent fractions that resulted in the answers on the grid.

Equivalent Fractions Bingo

		FREE		

Possible Answers

1/2	3/4	2/3	1/4	1/3
3/8	1/16	3/16	5/11	5/6
1/6	7/8	3/5	1/5	4/5
3/7	1/7	1/9	4/9	1/10
7/10	1/20	2/5	3/11	1/17

Equivalent Fractions Bingo

Equivalent Fractions (called out by teacher)	Reduced Form Answers
5/10	1/2
9/12	3/4
4/6	2/3
25/100	1/4
9/27	1/3
12/32	3/8
2/32	1/16
9/48	3/16
20/44	5/11
10/12	5/6
3/18	1/6
14/16	7/8
15/25	3/5
10/50	1/5
12/15	4/5
21/49	3/7
2/14	1/7
2/18	1/9
8/18	4/9
5/50	1/10
14/20	7/10
3/60	1/20
6/15	2/5
9/33	3/11
2/34	1/17

Directions: Answers are improper fractions. Randomly place each possible answer below on the grid after the teacher gives the equivalent mixed number for each improper fraction. If you win, identify the mixed numbers that resulted in the answers on the grid.

Mixed Number/Integer to Improper Fraction Bingo

		FREE		

Possible Answers

7/4	7/3	4/3	9/5	17/10
9/4	8/3	13/7	13/10	5/3
13/4	8/5	9/7	24/6	10/3
12/5	11/10	16/5	10/7	15/7
18/9	11/5	23/23	19/10	31/10

Mixed Number/Integer to Improper Fraction Bingo

Mixed Numbers/Integers (called out by teacher)	Improper Fraction Answers
1 and 3/4	7/4
2 and 1/3	7/3
1 and 1/3	4/3
1 and 4/5	9/5
1 and 7/10	17/10
2 and 1/4	9/4
2 and 2/3	8/3
1 and 6/7	13/7
1 and 3/10	13/10
1 and 2/3	5/3
3 and 1/4	13/4
1 and 3/5	8/5
1 and 2/7	9/7
4	24/6
3 and 1/3	10/3
2 and 2/5	12/5
1 and 1/10	11/10
3 and 1/5	16/5
1 and 3/7	10/7
2 and 1/7	15/7
2	18/9
2 and 1/5	11/5
1	23/23
1 and 9/10	19/10
3 and 1/10	31/10

Directions: Answers are mixed numbers. Randomly place each possible answer below on the grid after the teacher gives the equivalent improper fraction for each mixed number. If you win, identify the improper fractions that resulted in the answers on the grid.

Improper Fraction to Mixed Number/Integer Bingo

		FREE		

Possible Answers

1 and 3/4	2 and 1/3	1 and 1/3	1 and 4/5	1 and 7/10
2 and 1/4	2 and 2/3	1 and 6/7	1 and 3/10	1 and 2/3
3 and 1/4	1 and 3/5	1 and 2/7	4	3 and 1/3
2 and 2/5	1 and 1/10	3 and 1/5	1 and 3/7	2 and 1/7
2	2 and 1/5	1	1 and 9/10	3 and 1/10

Improper Fraction to Mixed Number/Integer Bingo

Improper Fractions (called out by teacher)	Mixed Number/Integer Answers
7/4	1 and 3/4
7/3	2 and 1/3
4/3	1 and 1/3
9/5	1 and 4/5
17/10	1 and 7/10
9/4	2 and 1/4
8/3	2 and 2/3
13/7	1 and 6/7
13/10	1 and 3/10
5/3	1 and 2/3
13/4	3 and 1/4
8/5	1 and 3/5
9/7	1 and 2/7
24/6	4
10/3	3 and 1/3
12/5	2 and 2/5
11/10	1 and 1/10
16/5	3 and 1/5
10/7	1 and 3/7
15/7	2 and 1/7
18/9	2
11/5	2 and 1/5
23/23	1
19/10	1 and 9/10
31/10	3 and 1/10

Directions: Answers are either mixed numbers or improper or proper fractions. Randomly place each possible answer below on the grid after the teacher gives an equivalent fraction for each of the possible answers. If you win, identify the mixed number, improper, or proper fractions that resulted in the answers on the grid.

Mixed Number/Improper Fraction/Proper Fraction Bingo

		FREE		

Possible Answers

9/12	5/9	2 and 7/8	10/4	7/12
12/5	4/7	11/4	20/25	18/16
4	5/10	14/7	3 and 2/3	5
7 and 1/6	9/10	4 and 1/2	3	1 and 7/11
9 and 2/3	20/16	5 and 3/10	1	6/18

Mixed Numbers/Improper Fraction/Proper Fraction Bingo

Fractions/Mixed Numbers (called out by teacher)	Equivalent Answers
3/4	9/12
10/18	5/9
23/8	2 and 7/8
5/2	10/4
21/36	7/12
2 and 2/5	12/5
16/28	4/7
2 and 3/4	11/4
4/5	20/25
1 and 1/8	18/16
32/8	4
1/2	5/10
2	14/7
11/3	3 and 2/3
40/8	5
43/6	7 and 1/6
18/20	9/10
9/2	4 and 1/2
12/4	3
18/11	1 and 7/11
29/3	9 and 2/3
1 and 1/4	20/16
53/10	5 and 3/10
19/19	1
1/3	6/18

Directions: Answers are fractions. Randomly place each possible answer below on the grid after the teacher gives the equivalent decimal value for each fraction. If you win, identify the decimals that resulted in the answers on the grid.

Decimal to Fraction Bingo

		FREE		

Possible Answers

1/2	3/4	1/5	1/3	1/8
3/8	1/4	1/9	7/9	2/3
3/5	4/5	1/25	1/20	3/20
3/25	2/5	1/10	7/10	1/100
9/100	7/20	7/25	9/10	5/9

Decimal to Fraction Bingo

Decimal Equivalents (called out by teacher)	Fraction Answers
.5	1/2
.75	3/4
.20	1/5
$.333\overline{3}$	1/3
.125	1/8
.375	3/8
.25	1/4
$.111\overline{1}$	1/9
.60	3/5
$.777\overline{7}$	7/9
.04	1/25
$.666\overline{6}$	2/3
.80	4/5
.05	1/20
.15	3/20
.12	3/25
.40	2/5
.10	1/10
.70	7/10
.01	1/100
.09	9/100
.35	7/20
.9	9/10
.28	7/25
$.555\overline{5}$	5/9

Directions: Answers are decimals. Randomly place each possible answer below on the grid after the teacher gives the equivalent fraction for each decimal. If you win, identify the fractions that resulted in the answers on the grid.

Fraction to Decimal Bingo

		FREE		

Possible Answers

.5	.75	.20	$.333\overline{3}$	.125
.375	.25	$.111\overline{1}$	$.777\overline{7}$	$.666\overline{6}$
.60	.80	.04	.05	.15
.12	.40	.10	.7	.01
.09	.35	.9	.28	$.555\overline{5}$

Fraction to Decimal Bingo

Fraction Equivalent	Decimal Answers
1/2	.5
3/4	.75
1/5	.20
1/3	$.333\overline{3}$
1/8	.125
3/8	.375
1/4	.25
1/9	$.111\overline{1}$
4/5	.80
7/9	$.777\overline{7}$
3/5	.60
1/25	.04
1/20	.05
2/3	$.666\overline{6}$
3/20	.15
3/25	.12
2/5	.40
1/10	.10
7/10	.7
1/100	.01
9/100	.09
7/20	.35
9/10	.9
7/25	.28
5/9	$.555\overline{5}$

Roman/Arabic Numerals Bingo

Roman numerals originated in ancient Rome and were the usual way of writing numbers throughout Europe into the late Middle ages. **Arabic numerals,** developed around the year 500, are the ten digits: 0, 1, 2, 3, 4, 5, 6, 7, 8, 9, based on the Hindu-Arabic numeral system, the most common system for the representation of numbers. Learning Roman numerals gives students a great appreciation for place value. When using Roman numerals, a number having only one place can represent a much larger quantity than an eight place number.

Example: MV = 1,005
CCCXXXVIII = 338

Note: There are never 4 of the same letter in a row. Therefore 4 = IV (5-1) 9 = IX (10 -1), 400 = CD (500-100), 900 = CM (1,000-100)

Conversion Table

Roman Numeral		Arabic Numeral
I	=	1
II	=	2
III	=	3
IV	=	4
V	=	5
VI	=	6
VII	=	7
VIII	=	8
IX	=	9
X	=	10
XV	=	15
XX	=	20
XXX	=	30
XL	=	40
L	=	50
LX	=	60
LXX	=	70
LXXX	=	80
XC	=	90
C	=	100
CC	=	200
CCC	=	300
CD	=	400
D	=	500
DC	=	600
DCC	=	700
DCCC	=	800
CM	=	900
M	=	1,000
$\overline{V}$	=	5,000

Directions: Answers are Roman numerals. Randomly place each possible answer below on the grid after the teacher gives the Arabic numeral.

Arabic Numerals to Roman Numerals Bingo

		FREE		

Possible Answers

V	X	IX	CD	DC
LXX	VII	IV	DCCC	M
CM	XV	XXV	XL	XVII
I	XIX	XLIX	CDL	CDX
DCCX	LXXV	CXC	CCX	LXXXVI

Arabic Numerals to Roman Numerals Bingo

Arabic Numerals (called out by teacher)	Roman Numeral Answers
5	V
10	X
9	IX
400	CD
600	DC
70	LXX
7	VII
4	IV
800	DCCC
1000	M
900	CM
15	XV
25	XXV
40	XL
17	XVII
1	I
19	XIX
49	XLIX
450	CDL
410	CDX
710	DCCX
75	LXXV
190	CXC
210	CCX
86	LXXXVI

Directions: Answers are Arabic numerals. Randomly place each possible answer below on the grid after the teacher gives the Roman numeral.

Roman Numerals to Arabic Numerals Bingo

		FREE		

Possible Answers to be placed in the grid:

5	4	90	52	25
17	7	77	520	2,010
29	87	221	40	159
67	101	312	800	243
762	76	105	420	3,490

Roman Numerals to Arabic Numerals Bingo

Roman Numeral	Arabic Numeral Answers
X - V	5
XX - XVI	4
L + XL	90
XL + XII	52
XV + X	25
XX - III	17
IV + III	7
LXXX - III	77
DXXX - X	520
MML -XL	2,010
XXX - I	29
LXXXV + II	87
CCXXX - IX	221
L - X	40
CLXX - XI	159
LX + VII	67
C + I	101
D - CLXXXVIII	312
M - CC	800
CCL- VII	243
DLX + CCII	762
L + XXVI	76
CC - XCV	105
CD + XX	420
MMMD - X	3,490

Game 11
PLACE CARDS – YOU'RE INVITED!

Materials
- Pencil
- Die or spinner displaying the digits 0 – 9
- **Place Value Playing** cards (pages 62-65)
- **Place Value Playing** sheet (pages 66-67)

Learning Standards for Mathematics
- Understanding place value of multi-digit numbers
- Read, write, and compare decimals

– Overview –

Students use their place value knowledge to create numbers. They then order the numbers their group has created.

– The Game –

This activity is for groups of up to 4 students. Give each group a deck of the **Place Value** cards and a spinner or die. It is preferable for the spinner to have a choice of numbers from 0 to 9. Give each student a **Place Value** sheet. The place value sheet has the following blanks:

________ __________ __________ __________ ________

The students fill in each blank with a number determined by the **Place Value** cards and the die.

Put the **Place Value** cards deck, face down, in the middle of each group. Decide beforehand how many blank places will be in the number. Add blanks or eliminate some blanks on the **Place Value** sheet if necessary.

Each student, in turn, rolls the die and chooses the top card from the **Place Value Cards** deck. The card the student chooses tells her/him the place in the number where the result from the roll of the die will be placed.

Remove any extra place cards from the **Place Value** cards deck if not playing with those places. Add extra cards if more blank places were added.

Example:

Top card says *Thousands Place.*
Throw of a die comes up with a 6.

The student enters a 6 in the thousands place on his **Place Value** sheet.

________ **6** __________ __________ ________

Depending on how many places are played for, the activity ends when one player has filled in all the places in her/his number on their **Place Value Sheet**. If a player chooses a card from the **Place Value Cards** deck and already filled in that place, her/his turn is over.

The **Place Value Sheet** allows for numbers up to 9,999,999. If helpful, put in commas before distributing the sheet or ask students to put in necessary commas. If you want to limit the size of the number, ask students to put an X in the unused blanks.

Example: **Place Value Card** chosen was "Thousandths Place"
Throw of a die comes up with a 6

____ ____ ____ ____ . ____ ____ **6**

a. Using decimal places, have the students put in the appropriate decimal point and include the **Decimal Place Value** cards deck (pages 64-65).

– Game Variations –

b. Play until everyone in the group has filled in all the places in her/his number. Order the numbers in your group in size order from least to greatest.
   a. What is the largest number in your group?
   b. How does it compare to the largest number in the class?

Questions for Further Discovery

1. What is the largest number that can be made?
   99,999
2. What is the smallest?
   11,111
3. What is the smallest or largest number using each digit only once? Put the numbers in your group in order from least to greatest.
   Answers will vary.

Place Value Cards

Ones Place	**Ones Place**
Ones Place	**Ones Place**
Ones Place	**Tens Place**
Tens Place	**Tens Place**
Tens Place	**Tens Place**
Hundreds Place	**Hundreds Place**
Hundreds Place	**Hundreds Place**
Hundreds Place	**Thousands Place**

Place Value Cards

Thousands Place	**Thousands Place**
Ten-Thousands Place	**Ten-Thousands Place**
Ten-Thousands Place	**Ten-Thousands Place**
Ten-Thousands Place	**Hundred- Thousands Place**
Hundred-Thousands Place	**Hundred-Thousands Place**
Hundred-Thousands Place	**Hundred- Thousands Place**
Millions Place	**Millions Place**

Decimal Place Value Cards

Tenths Place	**Tenths Place**
Tenths Place	**Tenths Place**
Tenths Place	**Hundredths Place**
Hundredths Place	**Hundredths Place**
Hundredths Place	**Hundredths Place**
Thousandths Place	**Thousandths Place**
Thousandths Place	**Thousandths Place**

Decimal Place Value Cards

Thousandths Place	**Thousandths Place**
Ten-Thousandths Place	**Ten-Thousandths Place**
Hundred-Thousandths Place	**Hundred-Thousandths Place**
Millionths Place	**Millionths Place**
Millionths Place	**Millionths Place**

Place Value Sheet

_____ _____ _____ _____ _____ _____ _____

_____ _____ _____ _____ _____ _____ _____

_____ _____ _____ _____ _____ _____ _____

_____ _____ _____ _____ _____ _____ _____

Decimal Place Value Sheet

Game 12
ORDER ME!

Materials

- Pencil and paper
- Index cards for **Order Me** sets

Learning Standards for Mathematics

- Fluency using the four operations
- Analyze patterns and relationships
- Operational fluency with fractions

– Overview –

The students must use their operational fluency, number sense, and mental math to arrive at a result that is another number in the distributed cards.

– The Game –

This activity is best done in groups of four or less. Each group is given a set of the fifteen **Order Me** cards. The sets of cards can be prepared on index cards by the teacher before the activity, or else each group may be given fifteen index cards, and one facilitator in the group may copy the numbers from the board. The numbers must be written large and bold. The object is to arrange the cards in equations so that using the operation(s) designated by the teacher (addition, multiplication, division, or subtraction), the group computes one of the other numbers in the card set. The students may use as many cards as they need to compute a result, but they may use a card only once. To finish, all cards in the set must be used in one of the equations.

Examples:

Operation: Addition

Cards are 1, 2, 3, 4, 5, 6, 7, 8, 9, 10, 12, 13, 17, 20, 21.

Possible Solution:

2 + 4 = 6
9 + 3 = 12
7 + 10 = 17
5 + 8 = 13
20 + 1 = 21

Operation: More Challenging Addition

Cards are 1, 2, 3, 4, 5, 6, 7, 8, 9, 10, 12, 14, 15, 21, 45.

Possible Solution:

4 + 1 + 3 + 7 = 15
10 + 12 + 14 + 9 = 45
8 + 6 + 5 + 2 = 21

Operation: Subtraction

Cards are 1, 2, 3, 4, 5, 6, 7, 9, 10, 11, 12, 15, 16, 17, 20.

Possible Solution:

12 - 5 = 7
9 - 3 = 6
17 - 2 = 15
11 - 1 = 10
20 - 16 = 4

Operation: More Challenging Subtraction

Cards are 1, 3, 4, 5, 8, 12, 15, 16, 20, 21, 25, 29, 32, 41, 46.

Possible Solution:

16 - 15 = 1
46 - 41 = 5
25 - 21 = 4
20 - 8 = 12
32 - 3 = 29

Operation: Multiplication

Cards are 2, 3, 4, 5, 6, 7, 8, 9, 10, 12, 20, 24, 36, 40, 63.

Possible Solution:

12 x 3 = 36
9 x 7 = 63
4 x 6 = 24
8 x 5 = 40
10 x 2 = 20

Cards are 1, 2, 3, 4, 6, 7, 8, 9, 10, 12, 16, 84, 96, 108, 160.

Operations: More Challenging Multiplication

Possible Solution:

4 x 3 x 9 = 108
7 x 6 x 2 = 84
8 x 12 x 1 = 96
10 x 16 = 160

Operation: Division

Cards are 2, 3, 4, 6, 7, 8, 9, 13, 18, 21, 24, 36, 63, 72, 91.

Possible Solution:

24 ÷ 4 = 6
63 ÷ 3 = 21
72 ÷ 9 = 8
91 ÷ 13 = 7
36 ÷ 2 = 18

– Game Variations –

a. Use All Operations

Cards are 0,1, 2, 3, 4, 5, 6, 7, 9, 13, 15, 16, 21, 22, 33, 41.

Possible Solution:
15 x 2 + 3 = 33
5 x 7 + 6 = 41
16 ÷ 4 + 9 = 13
21 + 1 - 22 = 0

More Challenging

Cards are 0, 1, 2, 4, 5, 6, 7, 8, 10, 17, 20, 23, 29, 42, 46, 70.

Possible Solution:
70 ÷ 10 x 6 = 42
4 x 7 + 1 = 29
46 ÷ 23 - 2 = 0
20 + 5 - 17 = 8

b. Use Fractions With Addition and Subtraction

Cards are 1/8, 1/6, 1/4, 1/3, 1/2, 2/6, 2/3, 3/4, 3/5, 4/10, 3/18, 5/6, 7/8, 7/12, 1.

Addition Possible Solution:
1/4 + 2/6 = 7/12 or 7/12 - 2/6 = 1/4, 7/12 - 1/4 = 2/6
2/3 + 1/6 = 5/6
3/5 + 4/10 = 1
3/4 + 1/8 = 7/8
3/18 + 1/3 = 1/2

Subtraction Possible Solution:
7/12 - 2/6 = 1/4
5/6 - 2/3 = 1/6
1 - 3/5 = 4/10
7/8 - 3/4 = 1/8
1/2 - 3/18 = 1/3

Game 13
WHERE SHOULD I PLACE THE NUMBER?

Materials
- Pencil
- **ABC** student activity sheets (pages 73-77)
- Index cards with integers in the interval appropriate for the grade level, one integer per card ***or*** a computer random number generator programmed for the number interval appropriate for the grade level
    - Internet sites for the random number generator
        - http://www.mathgoodies.com/calculators/random_no_custom
        - http://www.randomlists.com/random-numbers

Learning Standards for Mathematics
- Fluency using the four operations
- Interpret numerical expressions
- Analyze relationships between numbers
- Interpreting symbols

– Overview –

Students must interpret math vocabulary and symbols in order to strategize in which box to place randomly selected numbers. Students substitute the numbers in a mathematical expression given either in words or symbols. The aim is to get the highest possible result with the chosen numbers.

– The Game –

Distribute the appropriate **ABC** student activity sheet for your class level. Announce the interval from which the numbers will be chosen. Randomly choose a number from the appropriate interval. Each student must write the announced number in a box on the **ABC** activity sheet. After a number is placed in a box, it may not be changed.

Each row in the **ABC** activity sheet has a different result that is computed according to the instructions in the first column of that row. The instructions are either in words or in an algebraic expression.

Example: The number in column A is 9, column B is 5, and column C is 10. The algebraic expression in that row is A + B + C, compute the sum of 9 + 5 + 10. This sum, 24, is written in the **Result** column in that row.

Algebraic Expression	A	B	C	Result
A + B + C	9	5	10	24

After each of the fifteen numbers has been placed in one of the boxes on the sheet, the student computes the result for each row and sums the results for the Final Total. The student with the largest Final Total wins.

Example: Use the Activity Sheet #4 (page 76) and the interval 0-25.
The fifteen numbers called were in this order: 5, 11, 0, 16, 12, 6, 17, 9, 2, 13, 21, 10, 15, 20, 1

Algebraic Expression	A	B	C	Result
A + B + C	9	5	10	24
A x B x C	17	12	6	1,224
A x B	21	15	1	315
B x C	0	16	11	176
A x C	13	2	20	260

Final Total 1,999

Questions for Further Discovery

1. The largest final total of someone in the class is not necessarily the largest total possible. Using the chosen numbers, what is the largest final total possible?

   This will vary with the numbers called. A good strategy is to place the high numbers in the multiplication spots, with A x B x C having the highest numbers.

2. What is the smallest final total possible?

   This will vary with the numbers called. A good strategy is to place the lowest numbers in the multiplication spots, with A x B x C having a zero placed, if possible.

3. What was your strategy for placing a number?

   Answers will vary.

Student Activity Sheet #1
Where Should I Place the Number?

Instructions	A	B	C	Result
Add the numbers.				
Add the 2 largest numbers.				
Add the two smallest numbers.				
Subtract the smallest number from the largest number.				

Final Total ___________

Activity Sheet #2
Where Should I Place the Number?

Instructions	A	B	C	Result
Add the three numbers.				
Add the two largest numbers.				
Add the two smallest numbers.				
Subtract the smallest number from the largest number.				
Add the two largest numbers and subtract the smallest number.				

Final Total ____________

Student Activity Sheet #3
Where Should I Place the Number?

Instructions	A	B	C	Result
A + B + C				
A x B				
B x C				
A x C				
Add the two largest numbers and subtract the smallest number.				

Final Total ____________

Student Activity Sheet #4
Where Should I Place the Number?

Instructions	A	B	C	Result
A + B + C				
A x B x C				
A x B				
B x C				
A x C				

Final Total ____________

Multiplication/Division Student Activity Sheet
Where Should I Place the Number?

Instructions	A	B	C	Result
A + B + C				
A x B x C				
A x B ÷ C				
B x C ÷ A				
A x C ÷ B				

Final Total ____________

Note: This sheet may also involve decimals and/or fractions when computing the result.

Question for Further Discovery

How can you avoid getting a fraction in the result column? Is it always possible to avoid getting a fraction?

This is difficult. If A x B or B x C or A x C is even, you're lucky if you get a 2 as the divisor. Otherwise, in order to avoid a fraction as a result, you need a factor of one of the numbers being multiplied by the divisor.

Game 14
PRIMES, COMPOSITES, PERFECT SQUARES, FACTORS, AND MULTIPLES

Materials

- Pencil
- Graph paper
- Large graph paper for demonstration (optional)
- Dice or random number generator
  - Internet sites for the random number generator
    - http://www.mathgoodies.com/calculators/random_no_custom
    - http://www.randomlists.com/random-numbers

Learning Standards for Mathematics

- Fluency using the four operations
- Analyze patterns and relationships
- Gain familiarity with factors and multiples
- Understanding the categories of numbers: prime, composite, and perfect square

– Overview –

Students categorize numbers as either odd or even. This activity familiarizes the student with the categorization of numbers as composite, prime, or perfect square. It also familiarizes them with the concept of factor and multiple. Students are then able to analyze the characteristics of a number and place it in the correct category. The student gains an understanding of the significance of using math vocabulary to describe the different characteristics of numbers.

– A Preliminary Game –

Distribute graph paper to each student. Start with the following situation: A manufacturer of boxes was asked to create a box that would hold 24 jars of honey. He wants only boxes that are shaped as a rectangle or a square. If every square on the graph paper represents one jar of honey, draw all the possible boxes.

Students draw as many boxes that can hold 24 jars as they can on their graph paper. Ask students to describe the boxes they drew by telling the number of squares on each side of the box. Draw each one of these boxes on the demonstration size graph paper or regular graph paper.

There are 4 possible choices: 4 x 6 boxes, 3 x 8 boxes, 2 x 12 boxes, and 1 x 24 boxes

What do the numbers 1, 2, 3, 4, 6, 8, 12, and 24 have to do with the number 24? Introduce the words factors and multiples.

Each one is a **factor** of 24, and 24 is a **multiple** of each one.

A student may exclaim, "I have another – a 6 x 4 box!" Draw this one and cut it out of the demonstration graph paper or regular graph paper. Ask, "Is this really a different box?" Rotate it so it fits right on top of the 4 x 6 box already drawn on the demonstration graph paper. Explain this is a math concept called **commutative**, namely 4 x 6 = 6 x 4! Multiplication and addition are commutative operations.

Continue the conversation. The manufacturer now needs a rectangular or square box that holds exactly 11 honey jars. Draw all possible boxes.

> There is only one option: 1 x 11.

Draw this one on the demonstration graph paper.

Explain that 11 is in a special category of numbers called **prime** numbers and 24 is in a special category of numbers called **composite** numbers. A prime number has only 1 and itself as factors, while a composite number has factors other than 1 and itself.

Finally, the manufacturer needs a rectangular or square box that can hold 36 jars of honey. Students draw as many boxes as they can on their graph paper. Ask students to describe the boxes they drew by telling the number of squares on each side of the box. Draw each one of these on the demonstration size graph paper.

> There are five choices: 1 x 36, 2 x 18, 3 x 12, 4 x 9, 6 x 6.

Clearly, 36 is a composite number. Do you see a difference between the boxes you made for 24 and the boxes you made for 36?

> 36 can make a square box! 36 is therefore called a perfect square number.

The students now have a picture in their minds of each category of number!

– The Game –

Roll 4 dice or use a random number generator. The students use the numbers on the dice to create prime, composite, and perfect square numbers using one or more of the numbers rolled as a digit.

Example: The numbers rolled on the dice are 5, 6, 1, 4.
Prime numbers created: 5, 41, 61

There are three rounds. In Round One, the student is asked to create prime numbers. In Round Two, the student is asked to create composite numbers. In Round Three, the student is asked to create perfect squares. During each round, students write down as many numbers as they can in the designated category until the allotted time is up. Two to three minutes is usually sufficient time.

After each round, go around the room and ask each student to name a number she/he has written down. Each student who also has that number written down gets a point. If no one else in the class has the number, the student who suggested it gets two points.

Each student should have an index card on which to keep track of her/his score. This is a good time to use tallying. As students accumulate their scores, explain that keeping score in groups of 5 is so much easier when computing the final score. Look at the difference for a score of 12: **||||||||||||** **or** **卌 卌 ||**.

– Game Variations –

Factors and Multiples:

a. Create numbers that are multiples of one of the rolled numbers. Use 6 random numbers for this. Repeating numbers are allowed.

Example: Numbers rolled: 5, 6, 1, 4, 2, 2
Multiples of 4: 16, 56, 24, 12, 4

b. Use addition, subtraction, multiplication, or division to make a number in the designated category.

Example: Numbers rolled: 5, 6, 1, 4; Category: Prime Numbers
5 + 6 = 11
6 - 1 = 5
6 x 4 - 1 = 23

Questions for Further Discovery

1. Can you name any other perfect squares?
   1, 4, 9, 16, 25, 36, 49, 64, 81, 100
2. Are there any consecutive prime numbers?
   Just 2 and 3!
3. Are there any prime numbers that are two consecutive odd numbers? (These are called Prime Twins.)
   Examples: 5 and 7; 11 and 13
4. Multiplication is commutative. What about the other operations?
   $5 \div 4 \neq 4 \div 5$ Division is not commutative. $5 - 4 \neq 4 - 5$ Subtraction is not commutative.
5. Reverse the digits of a composite number (Example: 24 becomes 42). Is it still a composite number?
   Yes
6. Are there any composite numbers such that reversing their digits creates a prime number?
   Example: 91 and 19
7. What happens when you reverse the digits of a prime number?
   19 becomes 91, which is a composite number. 17 becomes 71, both are prime.
8. What happens when you reverse the digits of a perfect square?
   81 becomes 18, which is not a perfect square. 16 becomes 61, which is a prime number.
   36 becomes 63, which is a composite number.
9. Which prime numbers are still prime when you reverse their digits?
   73 and 37; 17 and 71; 31 and 13
10. Use the reproducible practice sheet (page 81).
    1. 75
    2. 9
    3. In row order: 19, 13, 29, 17, 11
    4. In row order: 63, 21, 54, 9, 72, 18, 48, 42, 75, 45
    5. 72, 48
    6. 75, 45
    7. In row order: 14, 21, 42, 28
    8. In row order: 50, 75, 45
    9. In row order: 63, 54, 9, 72, 18, 45
    10. In row order: 72, 44, 32, 16, 48, 52, 28
    11. 22, 26
    12. Divisible by 2

Student Practice Sheet

Primes, Composites, Perfect Squares, Factors, and Multiples

	63	14	26	19	21	54
9	13	72	29	44	32	
	16	17	18	22	48	42
50	75	52	11	45	28	

Answer the questions below using the above numbers. Circle the numbers you used. You may use a number more than once.

1. What is the largest composite number in the list above?
2. What is the smallest composite number in the list above?
3. List the prime numbers.
4. List the multiples of 3.
5. List the multiples of 12.
6. List the multiples of 15.
7. List the multiples of 7.
8. List the numbers that have a factor of 5.
9. List the numbers that have a factor of 9.
10. List the numbers that have a factor of 4.
11. Are there any numbers from the above list that you did not use?
12. What is a category that would include these numbers?

Game 15
FRACTION RECIPES

Materials

- Pencil and paper
- Die
- Multilinks or tiles in colors of red, green, blue, and yellow
- Color spinner with red, green, blue, and yellow.
- **Fraction Recipe** cards (pages 84-87)

Learning Standards for Mathematics

- Understand fraction equivalence
- Apply and extend understanding of multiplication to multiply a fraction by a whole number
- Understand addition and subtraction of fractions with like and unlike denominators

– Overview –

Students try to accumulate colored tiles in the amount that matches the fraction on their recipe cards.

– The Game –

This can be played in small groups or as a whole class. Multicolored cubes or tiles should be easily accessible for each student. Each student is given a **Fraction Recipe** card.

Example:

1/6 red 1/6 blue 1/6 yellow Rest green

A color spinner is spun and a die is tossed. Each student takes the number of tiles as shown on the die in the color shown on the color spinner. Continue until one student has the amount of tiles that match the fractions on her/his recipe card. If the student chooses, a player may decline to take the tiles on a particular turn. However, once a player takes the tiles, they may not be put back.

For the above recipe, a winning number of tiles would be:

24 tiles all together
4 red = 1/6 of 24
4 blue = 1/6 of 24
4 yellow = 1/6 of 24
12 green = rest of the tiles

– Game Variation –

If the game is played in small groups, all players may have the same recipe card. However each player takes a turn spinning the spinner and tossing the die and only she/he may use the color on the spinner and the number on the dice. In a group of four, two players may team up and each pair of partners shares a recipe card.

Questions for Further Discovery

1 What was your strategy for choosing the number of tiles you needed for each color? What did that strategy have to do with the denominators of the fractions on your recipe card?

Look for a common denominator. 1/2, 1/6, and 1/3 have a common denominator of 6. Any multiple of six tiles will be divisible by 2, 6, and 3. You can then form equivalent fractions to help determine how many of each color tile are needed.

Let's use 24 tiles. 1/2 = 12/24, you will need 12 red tiles.
1/6 = 4/24, you will need 4 yellow tiles.
1/3 = 8/24, you will need 8 blue tiles.

2 Why do these recipe cards not specify what color the "rest" should be?

1/2 red 1/6 yellow 1/3 blue	3/8 red 3/8 yellow 1/4 green

They already add up to one whole.
1/2 + 1/6 + 1/3 = 1
3/8 + 3/8 + 1/4 = 1

Fraction Recipe Cards

1/4 red
1/3 blue
Rest green

1/6 red
1/6 blue
1/6 yellow
Rest green

1/4 red
1/6 yellow
1/3 green
Rest blue

7/12 any color
1/12 blue
Rest green

1/4 blue
1/4 green
1/4 yellow
Rest green

1/2 red
1/2 blue

Fraction Recipe Cards

1/10 red 1/2 yellow 3/10 green Rest blue	1/2 red 1/6 yellow 1/3 green
1/8 red 1/8 yellow 1/4 green Rest blue	1/8 green 1/8 blue 1/4 red Rest yellow
2/3 red 1/6 yellow Rest blue	1/3 red 5/12 yellow Rest blue

Fraction Recipe Cards

1/5 red
3/10 yellow
Rest any color

1/3 red
1/8 yellow
1/4 green
Rest blue

3/8 red
3/8 yellow
1/4 green
Must have more than 20 tiles

1/3 red
1/6 yellow
1/2 green
Must have more than 30 tiles

5/9 red
1/3 yellow
Rest any color

7/10 red
1/5 yellow
Rest any color

Fraction Recipe Cards

1/4 red 1/2 blue Rest green	1/3 red 1/2 blue Rest any color
1/2 red 1/8 yellow 1/4 green Rest blue	1/3 red 1/6 yellow 1/3 green Rest blue
1/3 red 1/3 yellow Rest blue	1/3 green 1/6 blue 1/18 red Rest yellow

Game 16
BUILD WITH CUBES

Materials
- Pencil and paper
- Multilinks or other snap cubes
- **Build With Cubes** student activity sheet (page 89)

Learning Standards for Mathematics
- Understand equivalent fractions
- Apply and extend understanding of multiplication to multiply a fraction by a whole number
- Understand addition and subtraction of fractions with like and unlike denominators

– Overview –

Students use building ingenuity and a knowledge of fractions to build a cube structure.

– The Game –

Each student (or team of students) is given a challenge to create a structure using multicolored snap cubes. The student decides how many cubes in total to use. The amount of any particular color must be the given fractional part of the total number of cubes as instructed on the **Build With Cubes** student activity sheet.

Example: If the student used a total of 30 cubes and half must be red, 15 cubes in the structure must be red.

Each student must fill out the **Build With Cubes** student activity sheet to prove her/his structure follows the specifications. Watch the imagination soar in each student's creation! This activity makes for a great photo op!

– Game Variations –

a. Change the fractions for each color cube.
b. Give the students the number of cubes of each color and ask them to figure out what fraction each color is of the whole amount of cubes.
c. Give the students the structure they must build (example: a house) and compare the finished structures.

Questions for Further Discovery

1. How do you determine how many cubes in total you need?

   Look for a common denominator for the fractions 1/2, 1/6, 1/4 that is larger than 30.

2. How would you change this combination: 1/4 red, 2/3 yellow, 1/8 green, and the rest blue so it is possible to use?

   Using 48 cubes:

   1/4 = 12/48 12 red cubes
   2/3 = 32/48 32 yellow cubes
   1/8 = 6/48 6 green cubes
   50/48 50 total cubes But you are only using 48 cubes!

   You have to take away 2 cubes. Since 1/8 = 6/48 = 6 cubes, take 2 away from here. What fraction equals 4/48? 4/48 reduced is equivalent to 1/12. Exchange 1/8 for 1/12.

   1/4 + 2/3 + 1/2 = 12/48 + 32/48 + 4/48 = 48/48 = 1
   12 cubes + 32 cubes + 4 cubes = 48 cubes You did it!

Student Activity Sheet
Build With Cubes

Build a cube structure according to these rules:

1. You must use at least 30 cubes in all.
2. One-half of your cubes are red.
3. One-sixth of your cubes are yellow.
4. One-fourth of your cubes are green.
5. The rest of the cubes are blue

I used:

_____ Red cubes

_____ Yellow cubes

_____ Green cubes

_____ Blue cubes

_____ Total cubes

Game 17
FRACTIONS AND DECIMALS LET'S COMPARE!

Materials
- **Fraction Cards** (pages 92-131)
- Index cards for Decimal Cards

Learning Standards for Mathematics
- Understanding equivalent fractions
- Comparing the sizes of fractions with like and unlike denominators

– Overview –

Students use their understanding of equivalent fractions, relative size of fractions, and comparing decimals and fractions.

– The Game –

This game can be played with up to 4 students. Each student gets a set of the **Fraction Cards**. The cards are held with the fraction side up. On the back of each card are 60 circles. The fraction is represented by the black circles. If the fraction is 1/2, thirty out of the sixty circles will be black. Fractions that can be reduced have the word REDUCE on the back. Each front card sheet has 4 cards on it. Each front sheet is followed by a sheet with the corresponding backs for each card.

Example:

Front of Card

$$\frac{1}{2}$$

Back of Card

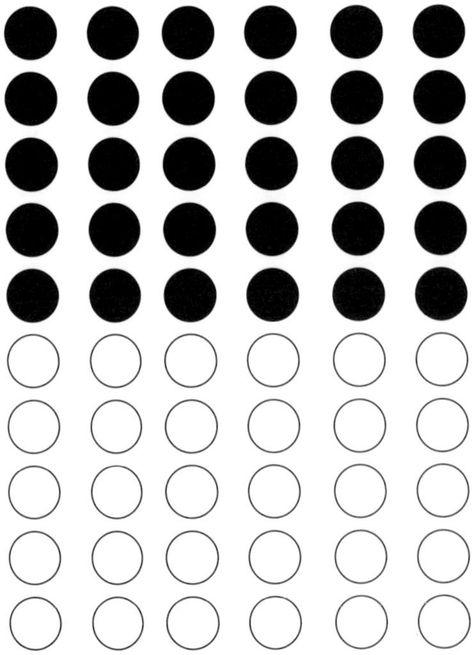

Front of Card

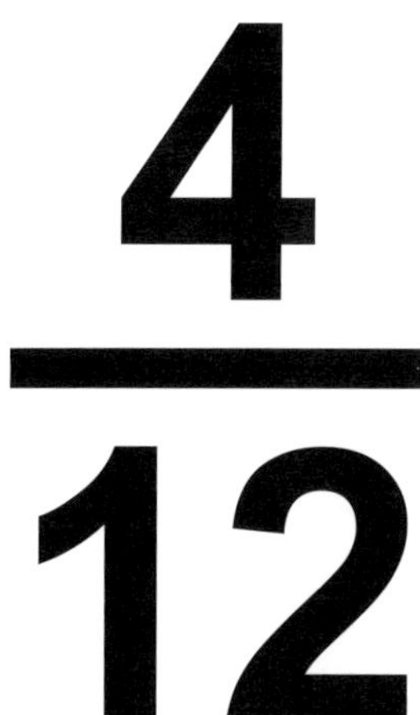

Back of Card

REDUCE

Students compare the topmost cards of their decks. The student with the largest fraction keeps all played cards. If there is a question about whose fraction is largest, flip the card to the back and compare the number of black circles.

If two students have cards with the same value, each shows the next card and whoever has the largest fraction gets the cards from both plays. The winner is the student with the most cards when the allotted time for the game is over.

This activity can be played with decimals. Have each student make her/his own set of decimal cards using index cards by converting each fraction from the **Fraction Cards** to a decimal. Play the previous activity with decimals.

– Game Variations –

a. Distribute several of the fraction cards and assign some to each student. On a blank card, ask each student to convert the fraction to a decimal.

b. Mix the fraction and decimal cards and play using both decks.

c. The fraction cards that are provided have fractions with denominators 2, 3, 4, 5, 6, 10, 12. These numbers are all factors of 60 and there are 60 circles on the back side of each fraction card. Fill in the reproducible blank front card sheets with fractions using 15, 20, and 30 as denominators. Fill in the spaces in the reproducible back card sheets with the amount of black circles that represent the fraction on the front. If the fraction can be reduced, write REDUCE on the back of the card.

Fraction Cards – Front

1

1

$\frac{12}{12}$

$\frac{11}{11}$

Fraction Cards – Back

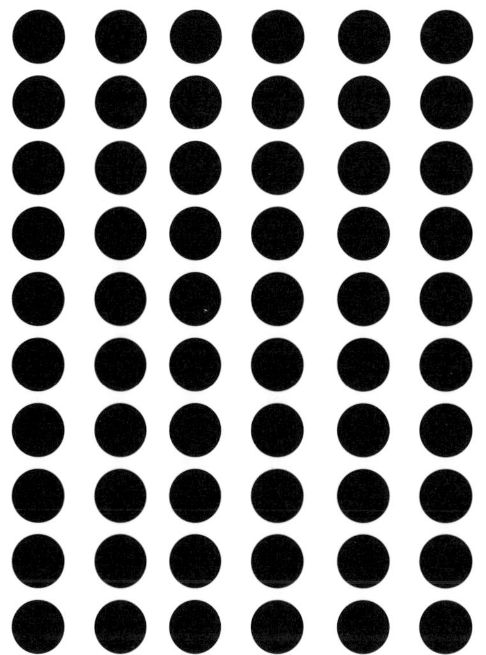

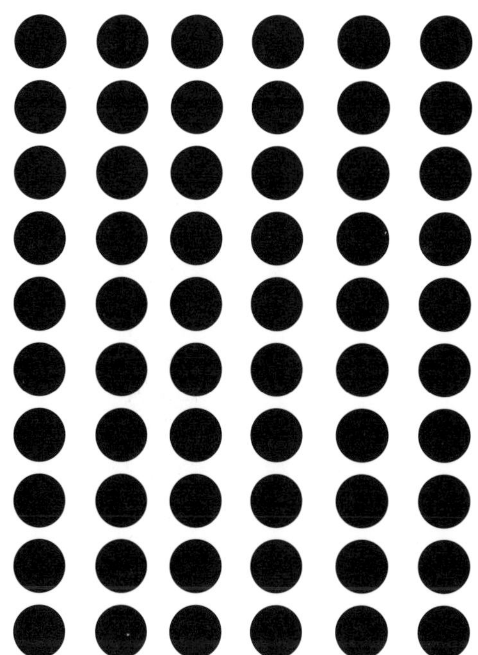

REDUCE

REDUCE

Fraction Cards – Front

$\frac{1}{10}$

$\frac{1}{10}$

$\frac{11}{12}$

$\frac{11}{12}$

Fraction Cards – Back

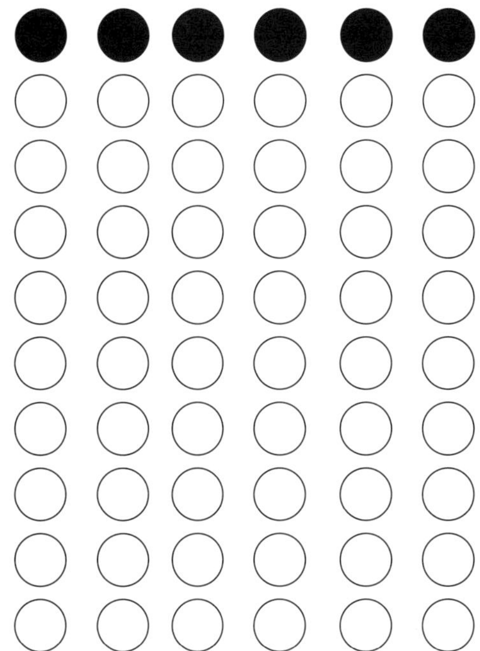

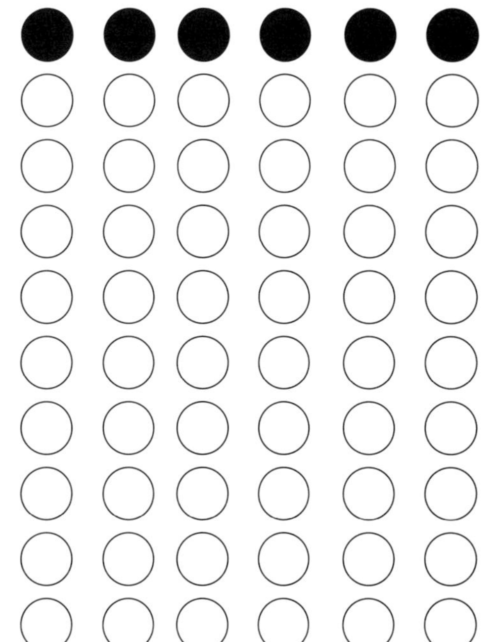

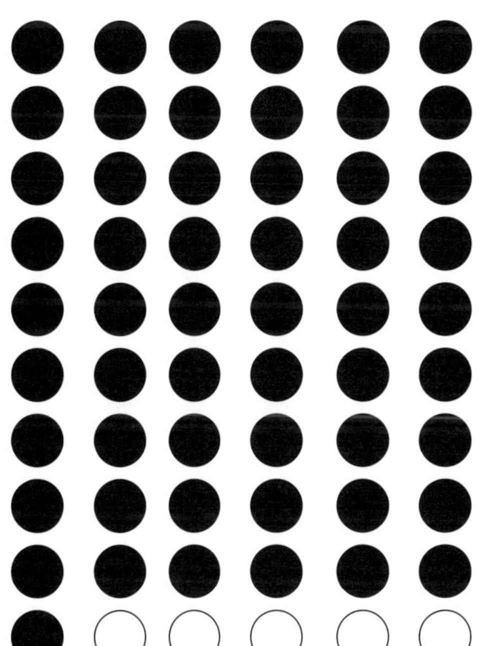

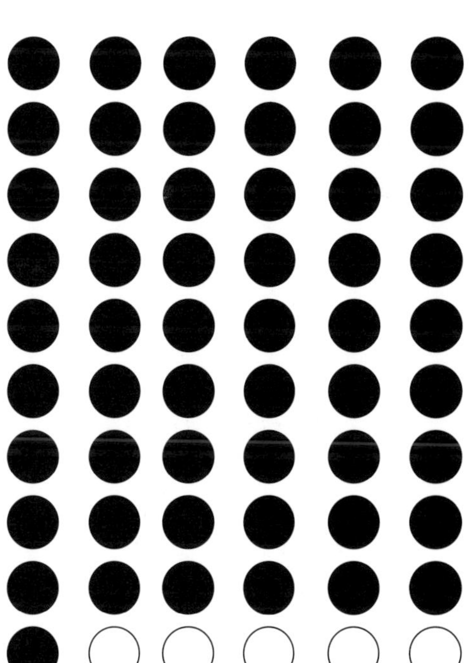

Fraction Cards – Front

$\frac{2}{4}$ $\frac{2}{4}$

$\frac{1}{2}$ $\frac{1}{2}$

Fraction Cards – Back

REDUCE

REDUCE

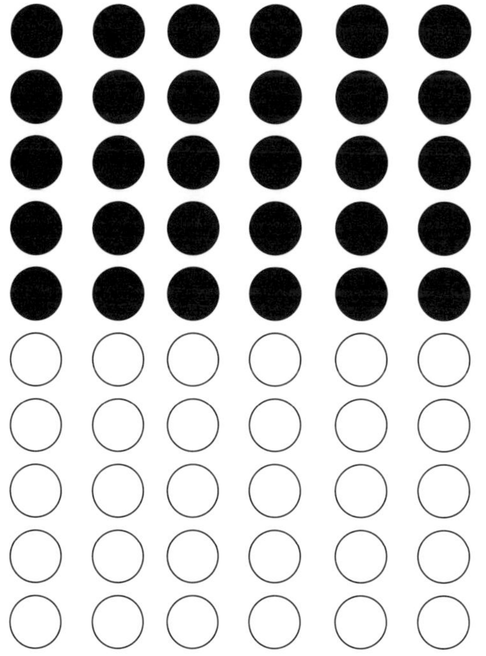

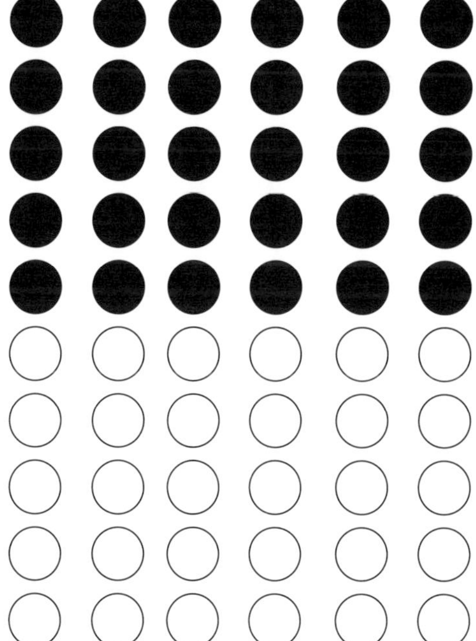

Fraction Cards – Front

$\frac{1}{5}$

$\frac{1}{5}$

$\frac{1}{6}$

$\frac{1}{6}$

Fraction Cards – Back

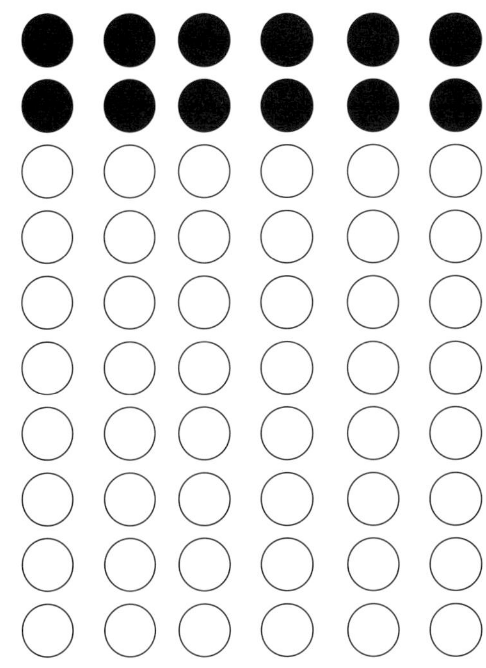

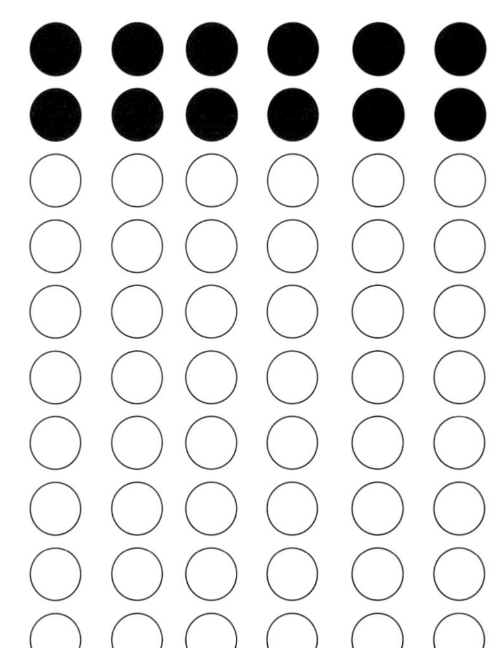

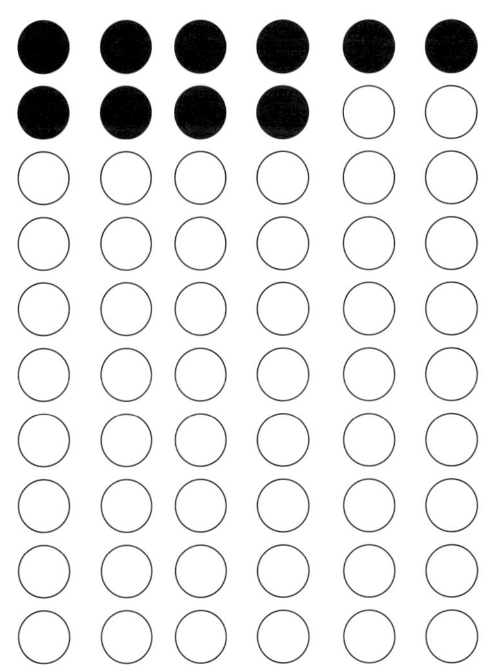

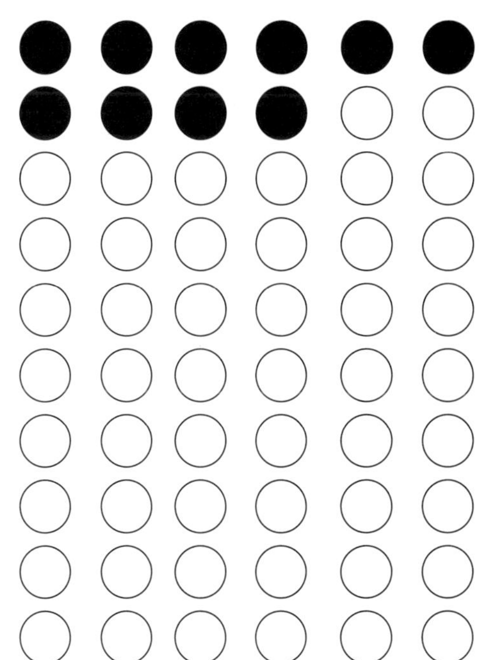

Fraction Cards – Front

$$\frac{4}{6}$$

$$\frac{4}{6}$$

$$\frac{5}{6}$$

$$\frac{5}{6}$$

Fraction Cards – Back

REDUCE

REDUCE

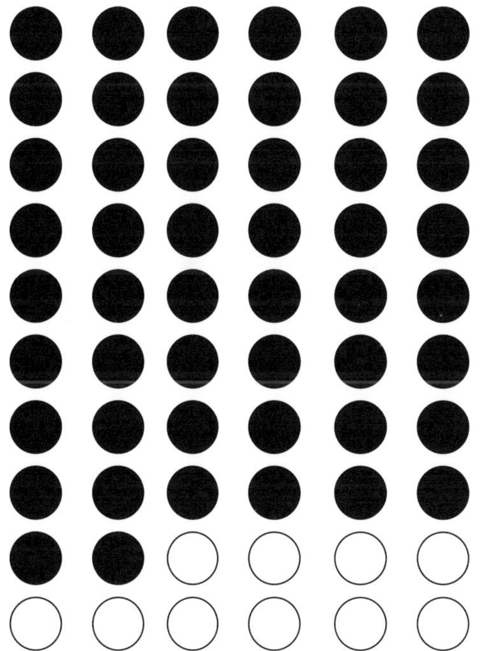

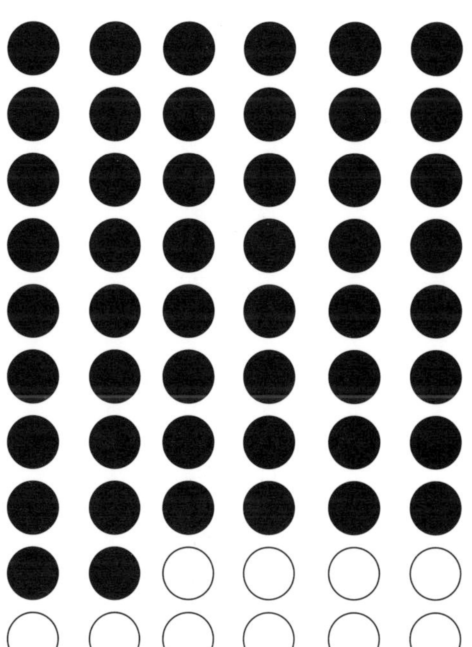

Fraction Cards – Front

$$\frac{1}{12}$$

$$\frac{1}{12}$$

$$\frac{1}{4}$$

$$\frac{1}{4}$$

Fraction Cards – Back

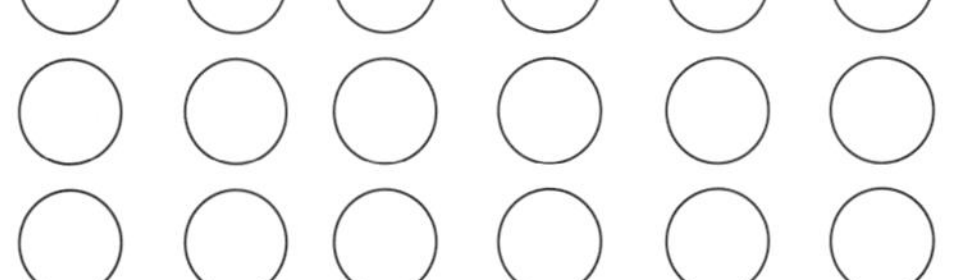
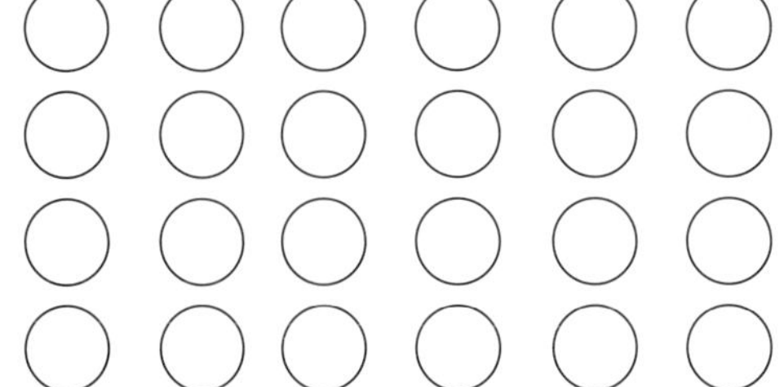
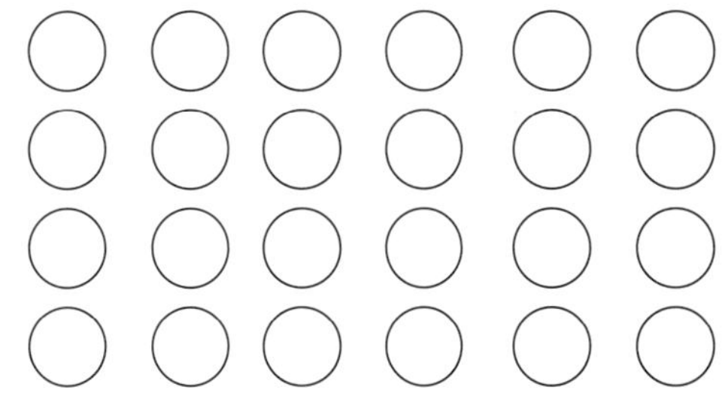
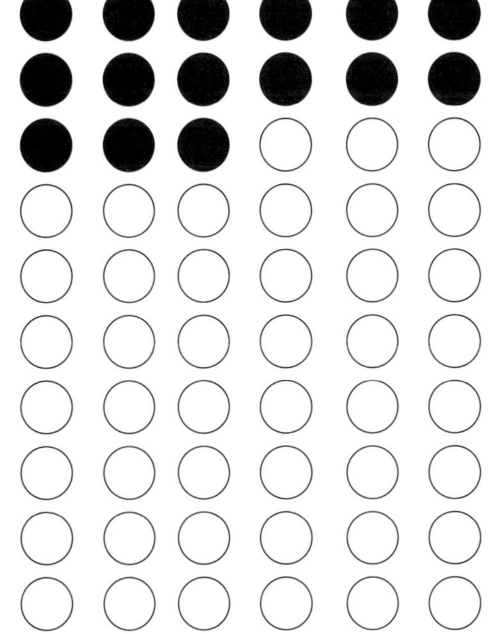
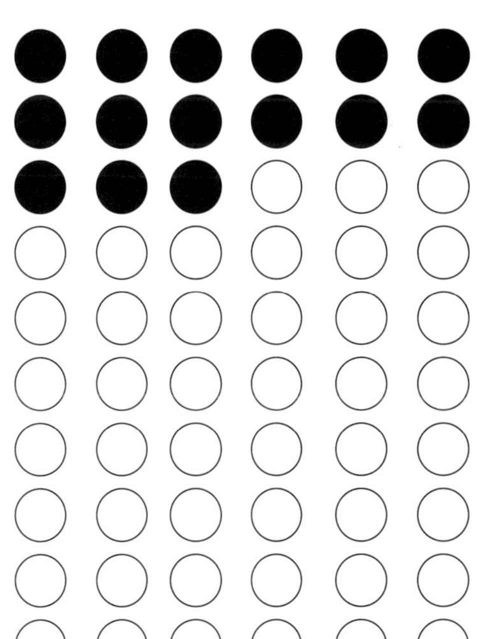

Fraction Cards – Front

$\frac{3}{3}$

$\frac{3}{3}$

$\frac{6}{12}$

$\frac{6}{12}$

Fraction Cards – Back

REDUCE

REDUCE

REDUCE

REDUCE

Fraction Cards – Front

$\frac{4}{12}$ $\frac{4}{12}$

$\frac{3}{10}$ $\frac{3}{10}$

Fraction Cards – Back

REDUCE

REDUCE

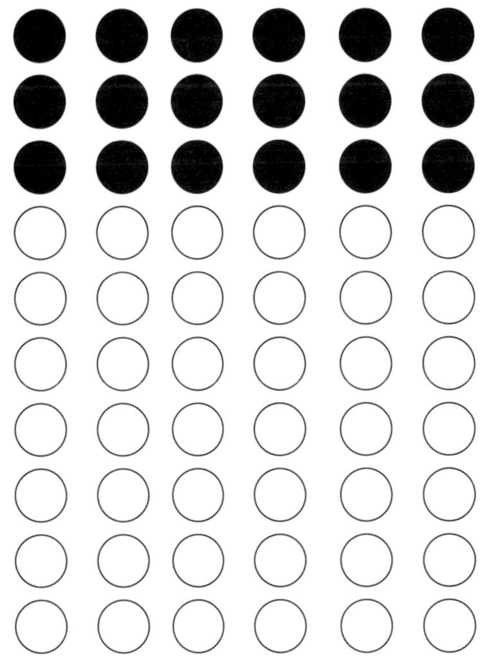

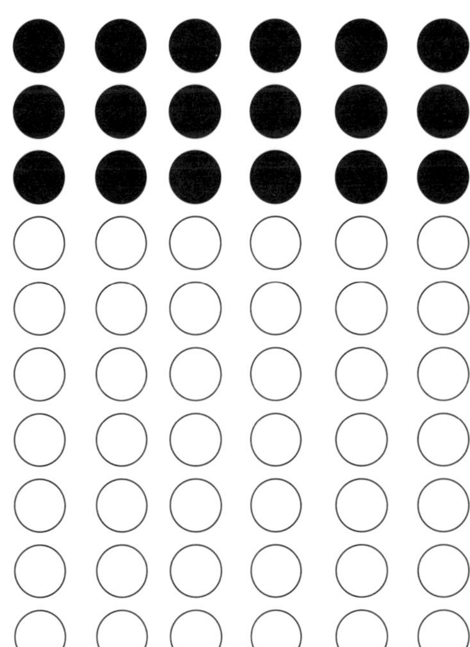

Fraction Cards – Front

$\frac{8}{10}$ $\frac{8}{10}$

$\frac{3}{5}$ $\frac{3}{5}$

Fraction Cards – Back

REDUCE

REDUCE

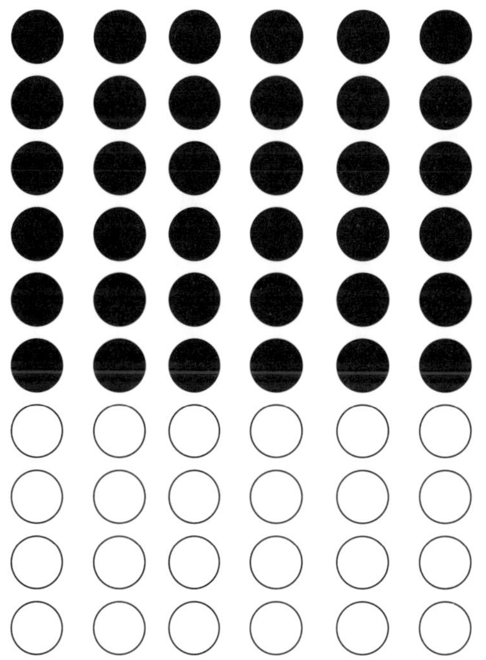

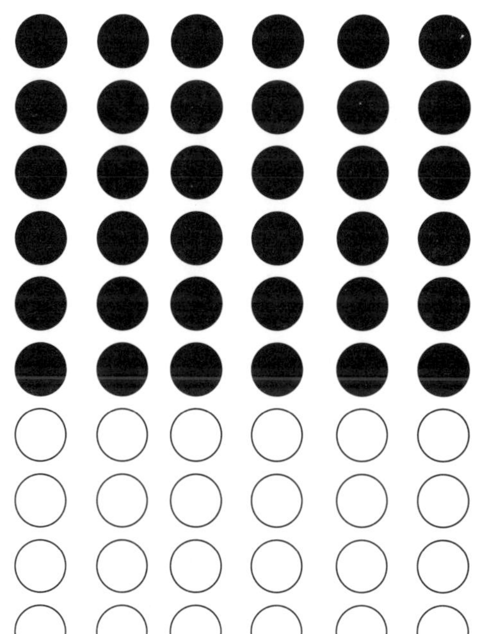

Fraction Cards – Front

$$\frac{3}{12}$$

$$\frac{3}{12}$$

$$\frac{7}{10}$$

$$\frac{7}{10}$$

Fraction Cards – Back

REDUCE

REDUCE

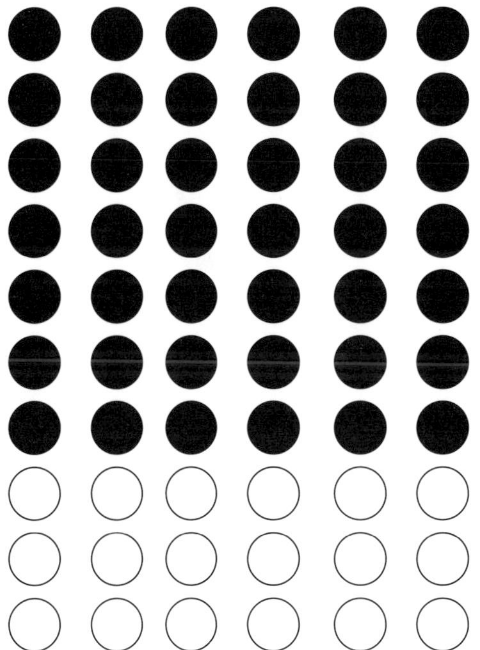

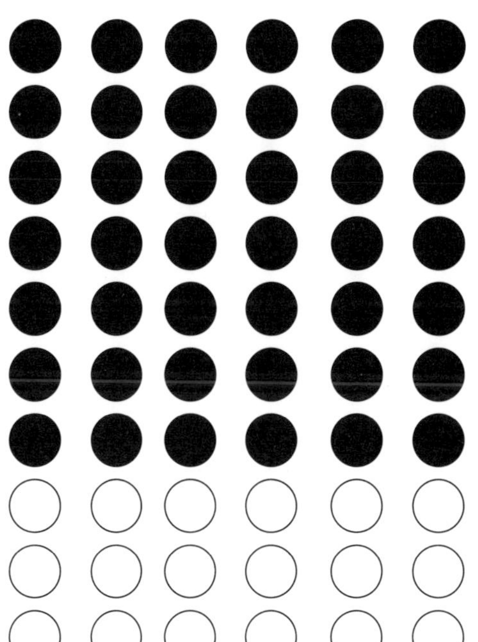

Fraction Cards – Front

$\frac{2}{3}$ $\frac{2}{3}$

$\frac{2}{12}$ $\frac{2}{12}$

Fraction Cards – Back

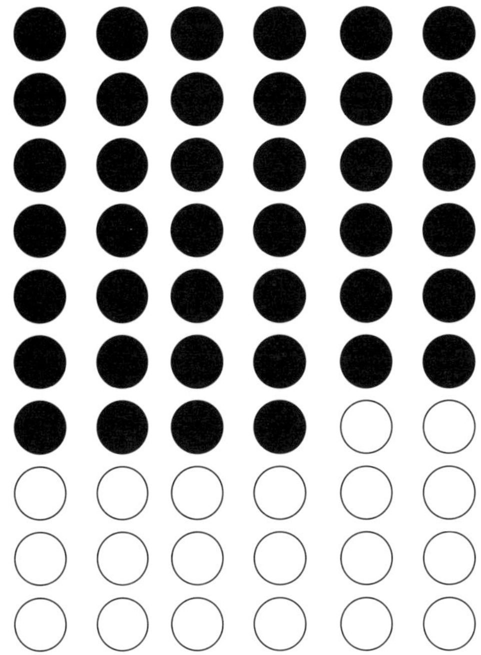

REDUCE

REDUCE

Fraction Cards – Front

$\frac{2}{5}$

$\frac{2}{5}$

$\frac{1}{3}$

$\frac{1}{3}$

Fraction Cards – Back

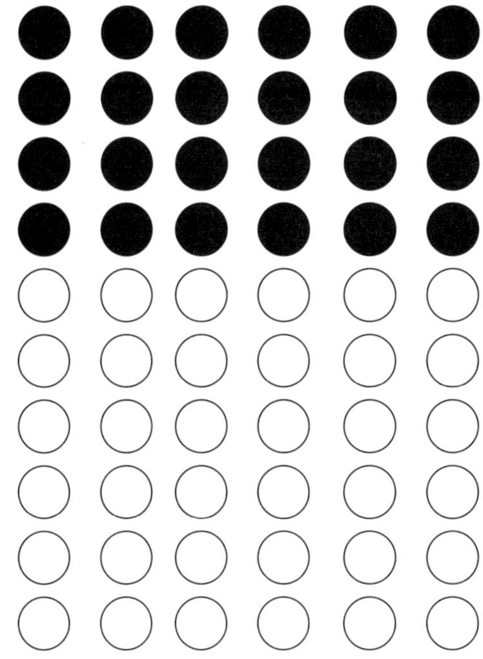

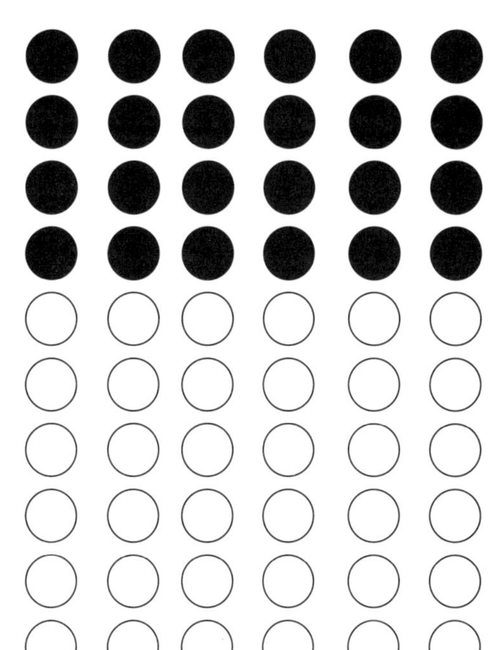

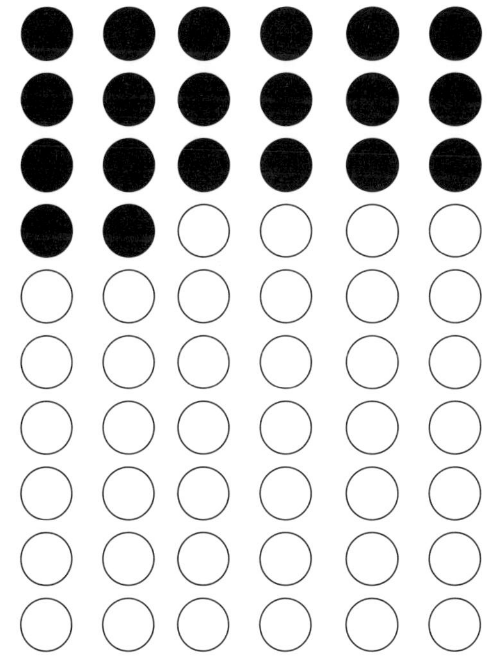

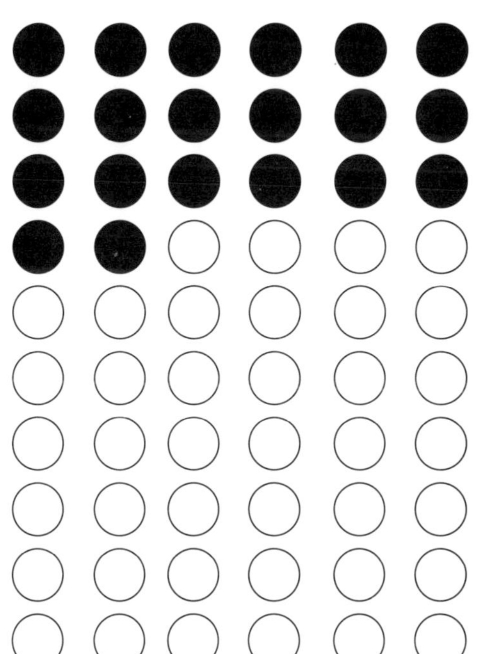

Fraction Cards – Front

$$\frac{9}{12}$$

$$\frac{9}{12}$$

$$\frac{4}{5}$$

$$\frac{4}{5}$$

Fraction Cards – Back

REDUCE

REDUCE

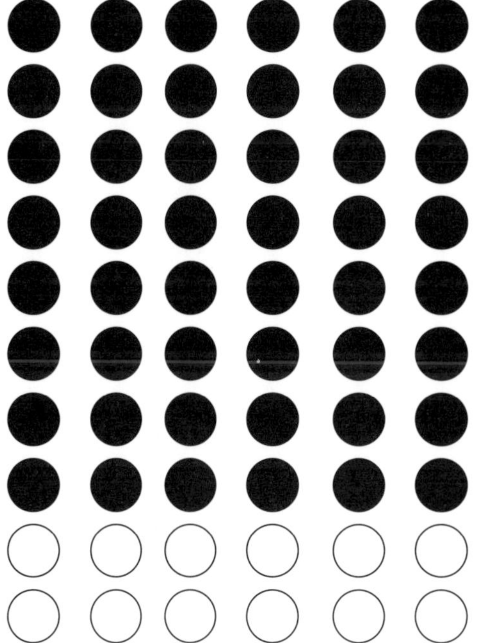

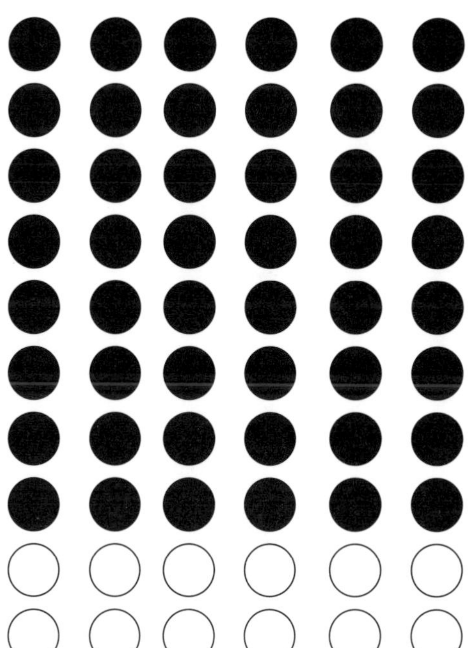

Fraction Cards – Front

$$\frac{5}{12}$$

$$\frac{5}{12}$$

$$\frac{3}{6}$$

$$\frac{3}{6}$$

Fraction Cards – Back

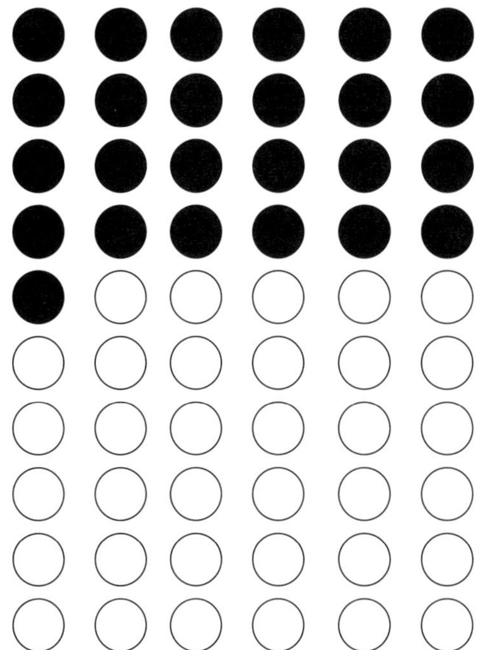

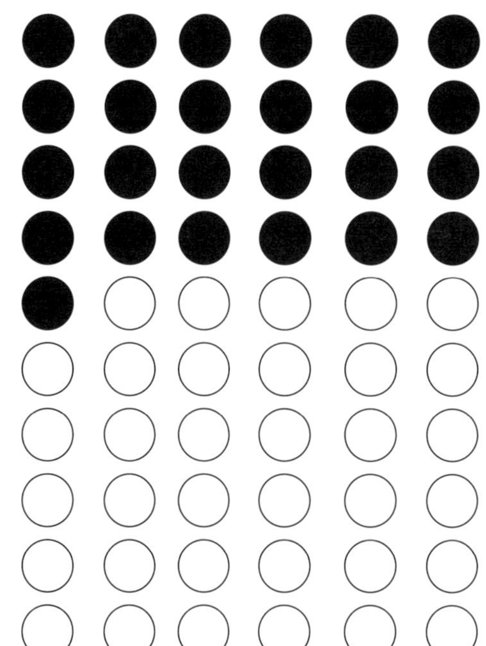

REDUCE

REDUCE

Fraction Cards – Front

$\frac{7}{12}$

$\frac{7}{12}$

$\frac{2}{6}$

$\frac{2}{6}$

Fraction Cards – Back

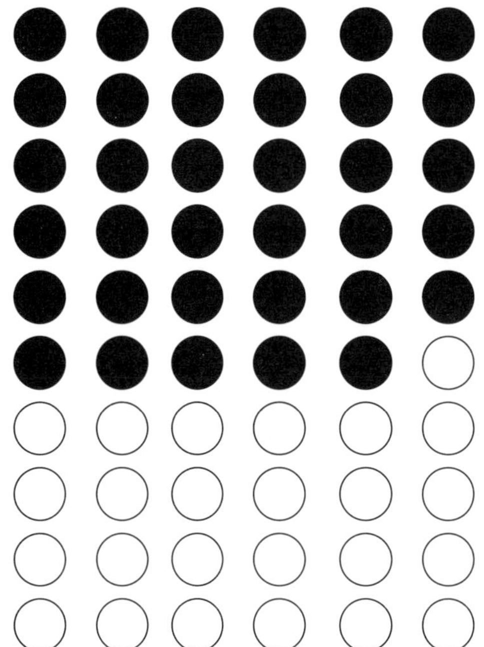

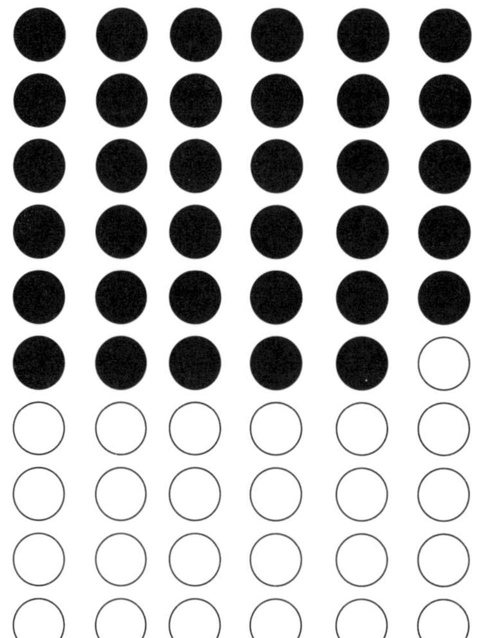

REDUCE

REDUCE

Fraction Cards – Front

$\frac{2}{10}$ $\frac{2}{10}$

$\frac{9}{10}$ $\frac{9}{10}$

Fraction Cards – Back

REDUCE

REDUCE

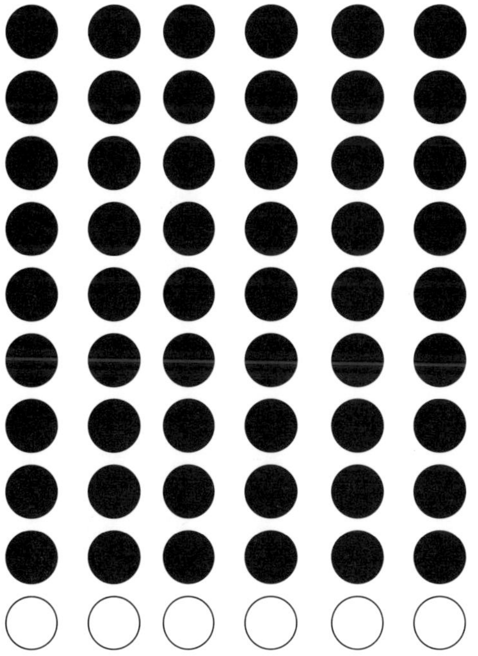

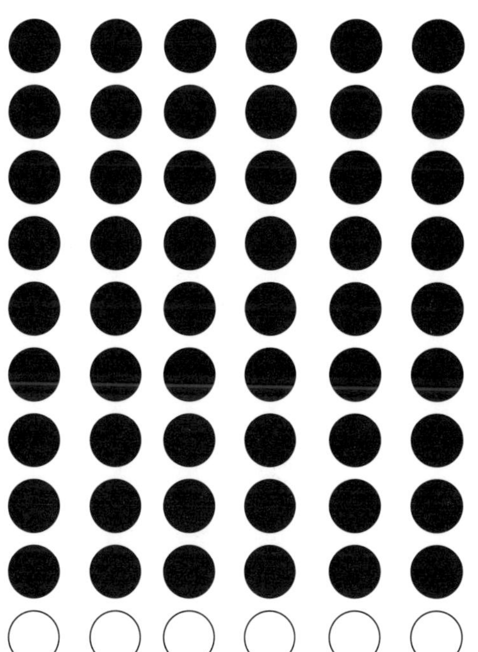

Fraction Cards – Front

$\frac{4}{10}$

$\frac{4}{10}$

$\frac{5}{10}$

$\frac{5}{10}$

Fraction Cards – Back

REDUCE

REDUCE

REDUCE

REDUCE

Fraction Cards – Front

$\frac{10}{12}$

$\frac{10}{12}$

$\frac{4}{4}$

$\frac{10}{10}$

Fraction Cards – Back

REDUCE

REDUCE

REDUCE

REDUCE

Fraction Cards – Front

$$\frac{6}{10}$$

$$\frac{6}{10}$$

$$\frac{5}{5}$$

$$\frac{2}{2}$$

Fraction Cards – Back

REDUCE REDUCE

REDUCE REDUCE

Fraction Cards – Front

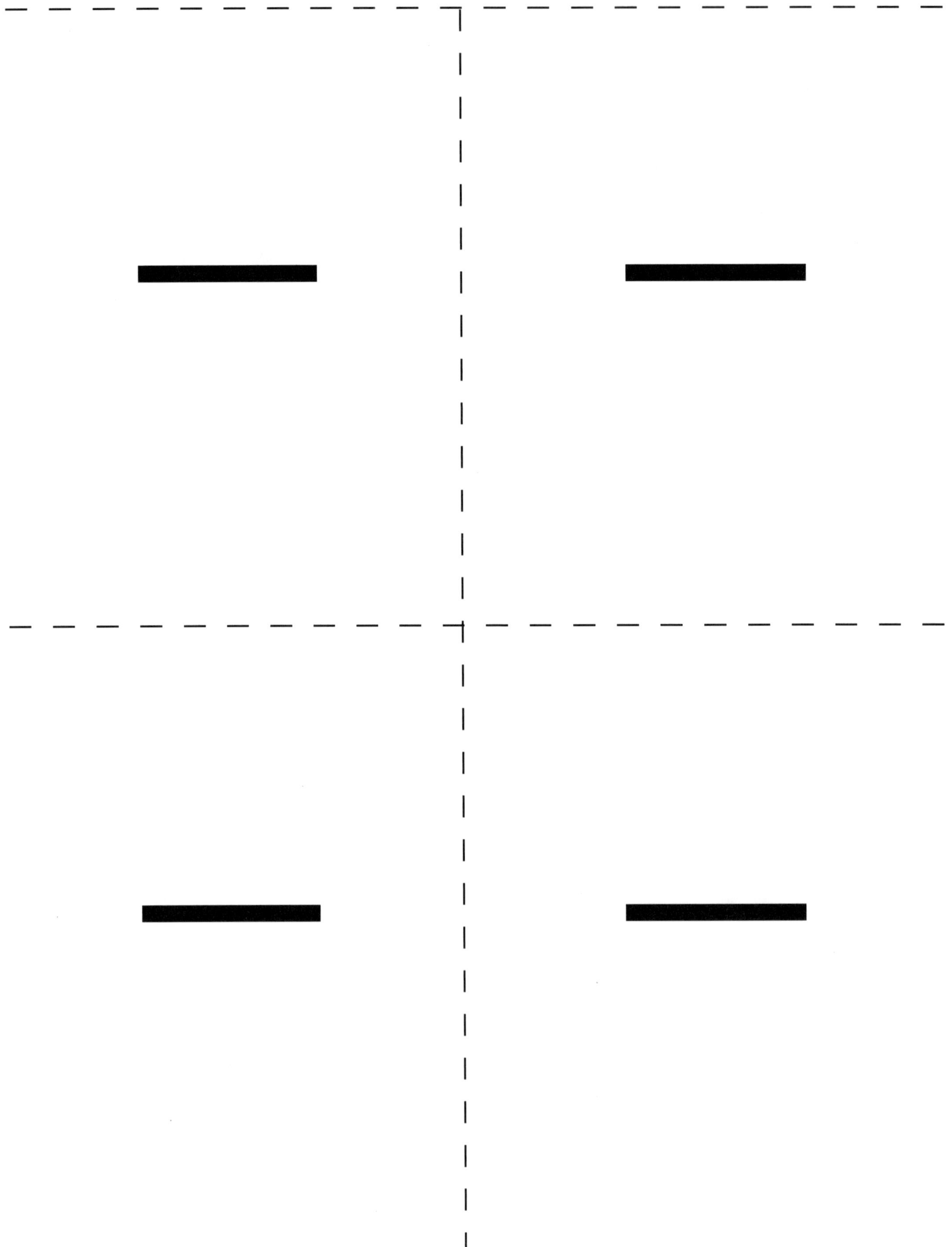

Fraction Cards – Back

Game 18
CLOTHESLINE FRACTIONS/DECIMALS

Materials
- String or clothesline
- Clothespins or paper clips
- Fraction Cards (pages 92-131)
- Decimal Cards (student's index cards)

Learning Standards for Mathematics
- Understanding equivalent fractions
- Placing fractions on a number line

– Overview –

This activity gives the students practice comparing fractions and/or decimals by asking them to order the numbers on a number line.

– The Game –

Using the Fraction Cards from the **Fraction/Decimal Card Game**, distribute one card and one clothespin or paper clip to each student in the class. Attach a string or clothesline across the room. Attach a card with "0" on one end of the string and a card with "1" on the other end. Ask each student to attach her/his card on the line in the size order. Equivalent fractions should be attached to each other.

Break the class up into partners. Ask each pair to choose two fractions that are next to each other on the class number line. They now need to come up with a fraction that is in-between these two fractions. Without telling the class which two fractions they originally chose, the pair announces the “in-between” fraction. The students must try to figure out which two fractions it is in-between and write the fractions down. After calling time, one point goes to every pair that correctly identifies the two fractions.

– Game Variations –

a. Mix decimal and fraction cards and attach the cards to the number line. Continue with the same activity explained above.

b. Break the class up into groups of ten. Randomly choose ten cards from either the fraction, decimal, or both cards and give each group the 10 cards. Each student in the group gets one of the cards. Ask them to arrange themselves in a horizontal line according to the card they received, from smallest to largest. Make sure the card they have is facing outward, so the rest of the class can see if they agree or disagree with the order. This is a great photo op!

Game 19
MAKE 1

Materials
- 4 dice (ten-sided dice if available)
- **Make 1** student activity sheet (page 134)

Learning Standards for Mathematics
- Understanding equivalent fractions
- Comparing the sizes of different fractions
- Solve a problem involving addition and subtraction of fractions

– Overview –

Students strategize to come up with four fractions whose sum is closest to 1.

– The Game –

Roll 4 dice. Students, using the numbers on the dice, create a proper fraction. To create the denominator or numerator, the student may use any of the numbers shown.

Example: After a roll of the four dice the numbers are: **4**, **6**, **2**, **1**. Any of these numbers may be the denominator or the numerator. The choices are 1/2, 1/4, 1/6, 2/6, or 2/4.

After four rolls of the four dice, students sum the fractions they created after each roll. Whoever has the closest to 1 or equal to 1 at the end of 4 throws is the winner. You may go over 1.

Example:		
First throw	1, 3, 2, 4	fraction created 1/4
Second throw	2, 4, 5, 1	fraction created 1/4
Third throw	5, 5, 5, 2	fraction created 2/5
Fourth throw	1, 2, 6, 3	fraction created 1/6

Total 1/4 + 1/4 + 2/5 + 1/6 = 15/60 + 15/60 + 24/60 + 10/60 = 64/60

– Game Variations –

To create the denominator you may add, subtract, multiply, or divide any two of the numbers thrown on the 4 dice. You may use each number only once.

Example: First throw: **1**, **3**, **2**, **4**
Possible fractions: 1/3, 1/2, 1/4, 2/3, 3/4, 2/4
Using the extension, you may also compute the following as a denominator:

$\frac{1}{6}$ 2 x 3 = 6 The possible fractions would then be 1/6 or 4/6.

$\frac{1}{8}$ 2 x 4 = 8 The possible fractions would then be 1/8 or 3/8.

$\frac{1}{5}$ 3 + 2 = 5 The possible fractions would then be 1/5 or 4/5.

Questions for Further Discovery

Who thinks her/his sum came the closest to 1? Compare the relative sizes of the answers. Using the numbers we threw on the dice, could someone have come closer to 1?

Yes! 1/4 + 1/5 + 2/5 + 1/6 = 15/60 + 12/60 + 24/60 + 20/60 = 61/60!

Student Activity Sheet

Numbers Rolled on Dice	Fraction
Total	

Computation Space

Game 20
TEACHABLE MOMENTS

What Makes a Number Odd or Even?

What is the difference between an even and odd number? Many students will recite the twos times table. Ask them for other ways to describe an even number. One response might be, “The ones digit is either 0, 2, 4, 6, or 8.”

An important definition of an even number is that it can be broken up into pairs with no remainder, while an odd number always leaves one remaining “pairless” when broken into pairs.

Understanding this concept is important when discussing why an odd number plus (or minus) an odd number is an even number, while an even number plus (or minus) an odd number is an odd number. It is also necessary for understanding why an odd number multiplied by an odd number results in an odd number, while the product of an even number and an odd number results in an even number.

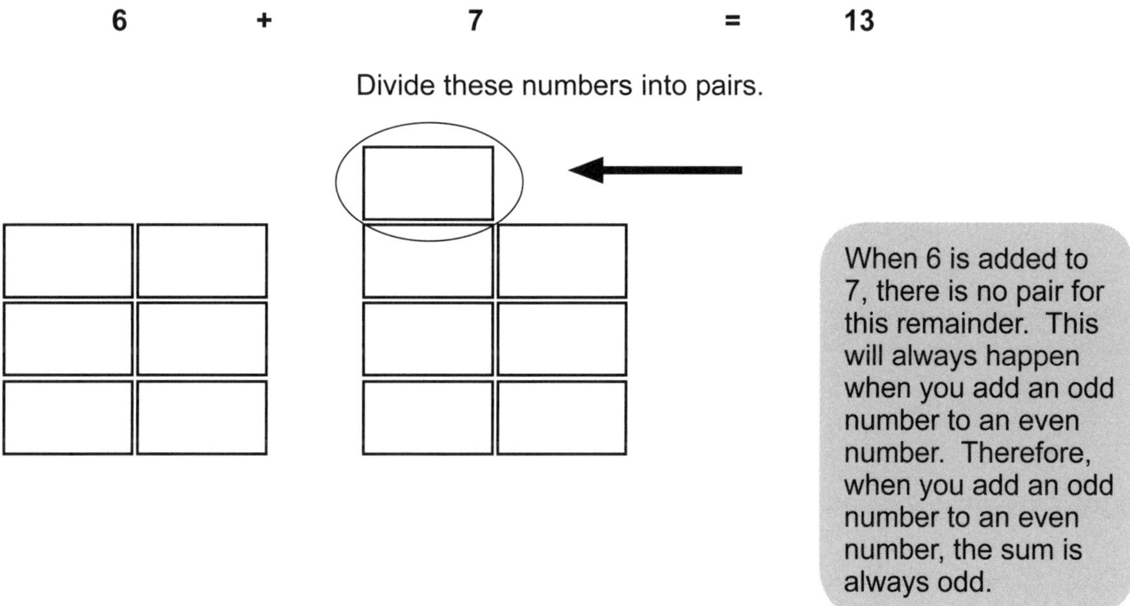

However, **5** **+** **7** **=** **12**

When 5 is added to 7, the two remainders make up a pair and the sum is an even number. Therefore, when you add an odd number to an odd number the sum is even.

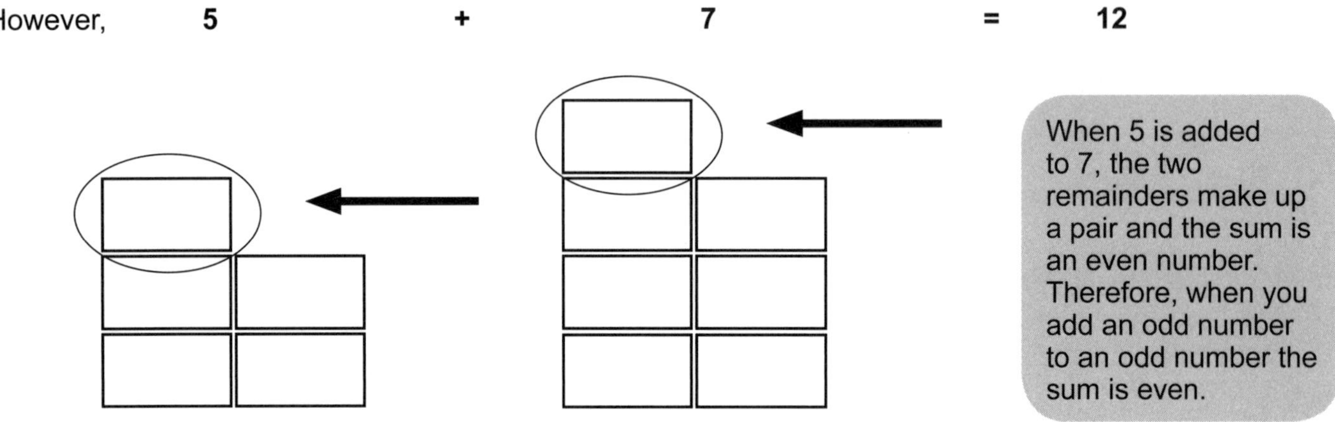

Similarly, when an odd number is multiplied by an odd number, there is always an odd number of “pairless” ones. When an odd number is multiplied by an even number, there is an even number of “pairless” ones, and they can be made into pairs.

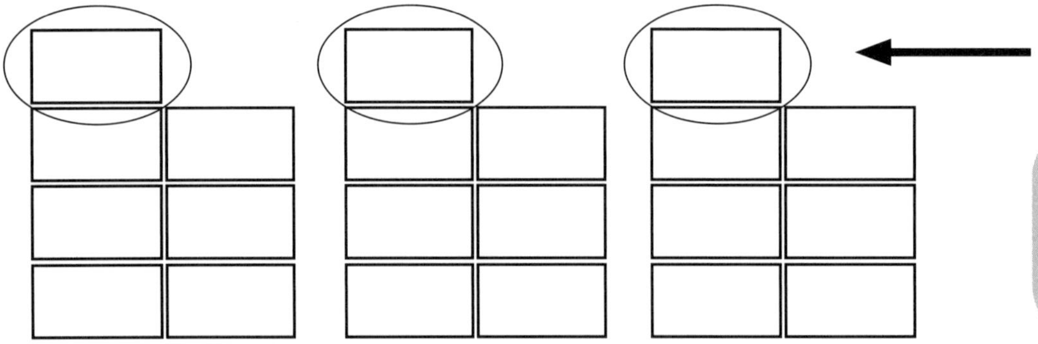

3 x 7 = 21

A pair can be made, but there is one that remains "pairless."

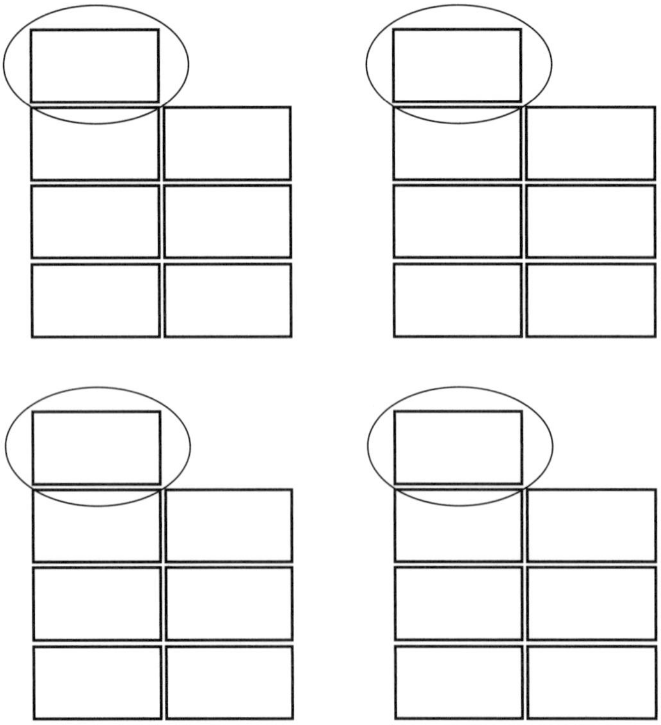

4 x 7 = 28

The four "pairless" ones can be made into pairs.

Divisibility Rules

When playing these games many students want to quickly know if a number is divisible by 3. This is a good point to review or introduce divisibility rules. (See **Divisibility Rules Chart** on page 140). The rule for divisibility by 3 is: Add the digits of the number and see if that sum is divisible by 3.

Why Does the Divisibility Rule for 3 Work?
Is this a trick, like hocus pocus or is there logic to it? To understand this rule, you have to understand the question that division answers. How many groups of 3 are in the number? If there is an even number of groups of 3 and no remainder, the number is divisible by 3.

- When 1,000 is divided by 3, there are 333 groups of three and 1 remainder.
- When 100 is divided by 3, there are 33 groups of 3 and 1 remainder.
- When 10 is divided by 3, there are 3 groups of three and 1 remainder.
- When any power of 10 (10^x) is divided by 3, there is always a remainder of 1.

Let's examine the number **123**.

100 + 20 + 3 = 123
100 + 10 + 10 + 3

Divide each component by 3.

- 100 divided by 3 has 1 remainder.
  20 = 10 + 10. Each ten divided by 3 has 1 remainder; therefore 20 divided by 3 has 2 remainders. There are **also** 3 ones.
- Add all these remainders and the 3 ones and to see if you can make groups of 3.

1 + 2 + 3 = 6. 6 is divisible by 3. Therefore the number 123 can be made into groups of three with no remainders!

Since dividing any power of 10 by 3 always gives 1 as the remainder, adding the digits of any given number gives us the sum of all the remainders after we have made groups of 3 plus the number of ones. If this sum is divisible by three, then the given number can be made into groups of three with no remainder. It is therefore divisible by 3! (See next page.)

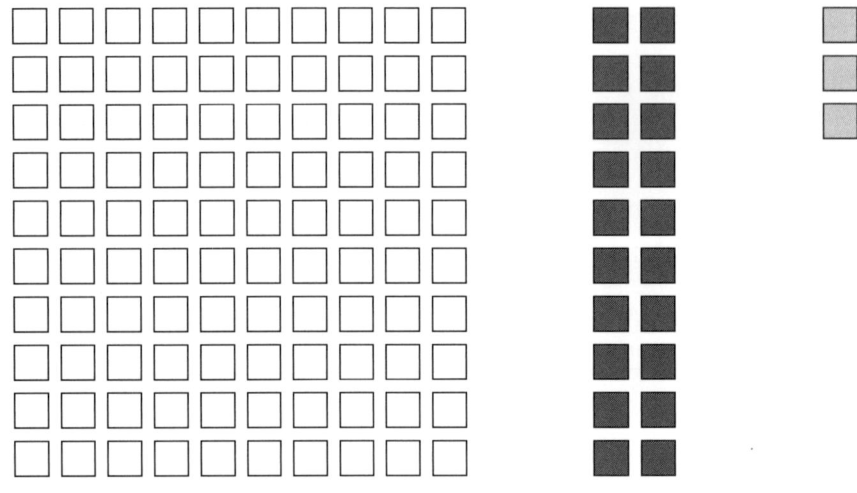

100 + 20 + 3 = 123

1 remainder when 100 is divided by 3

1 remainder when 10 is divided by 3

3 ones

Can groups of three be made out of these?

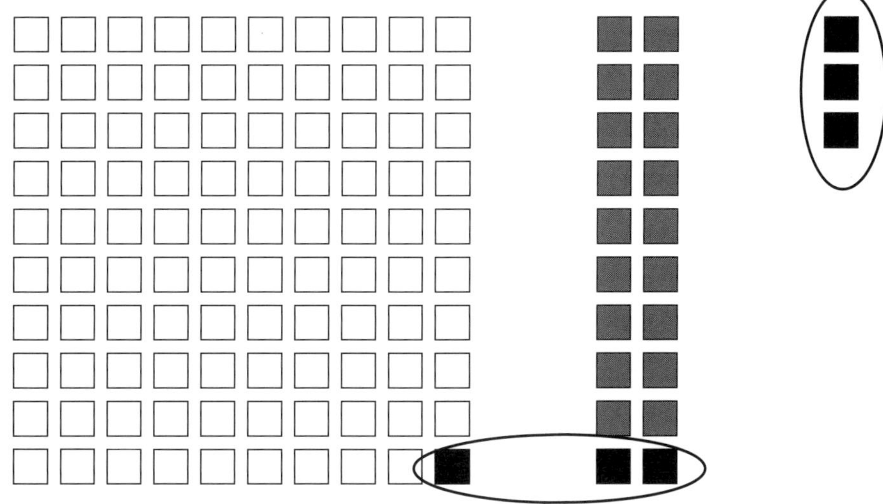

Yes, so 123 is divisible by 3. 1 + 2 + 3 = 6, 6 is divisible by 3!

What about **124**?

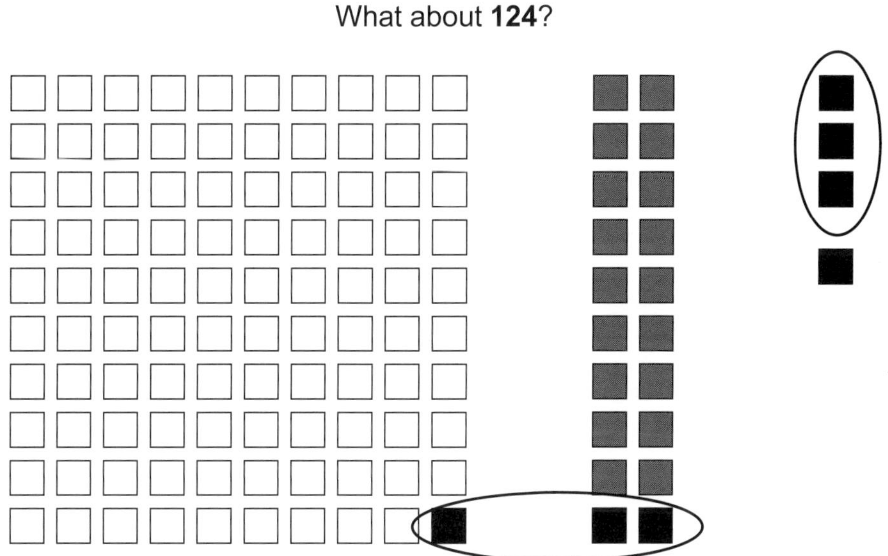

When groups of 3 are made, there is 1 remainder. Therefore 124 is not divisible by 3.

124 ÷ 3 = 41 groups of 3 with <u>1 remainder</u>.
1 + 2 + 4 = 7; 7 ÷ 3 = 2 groups of 3 and <u>1 remainder</u>.

If the number is not divisible by 3, there will be a remainder when you divide the sum of the digits.
Is 124 divisible by 3?

- 1 + 2 + 4 = 7. 7 divided by 3 is 2 groups of 3 and 1 remainder. This means that 124 is not divisible by 3, and when it is divided by 3, there will be a remainder of 1!

The same rule applies to 9. If the sum of the digits of the number is divisible by 9, the number is divisible by 9. It works for the same reason. Every power of 10 when divided by 9 has a remainder of 1.

Divisibility Rules Chart

Number	Divisibility Rule
2	Even number
3	Sum of the digits is divisible by 3
4	The 2-digit number in the tens and ones place is divisible by 4. Example: 124 is divisible by 4 because 24 is divisible by 4. 126 is not divisible by 4 because 26 is not divisible by 4.
5	Ones place is a 5 or 0.
6	Even number that is divisible by 3
8	If the hundreds place is an even number, test if the 2-digit number in the tens and ones place is divisible by 8. 416 is divisible by 8 because 16 is divisible by 8. If the number in the hundreds place is odd, add 4 to the 2-digit number in the tens and ones place. Example: 1516 is not divisible by 8 because 4 + 16 = 20 and 20 is not divisible by 8.
9	Sum of the digits is divisible by 9
10	Ones place is a 0.

Why Do the Divisibility Rules for 4 and 8 Work?

As with divisibility by 3, to prove a number is divisible by 4 or 8, check to see if you can make groups of 4 or 8 with no remainders.

4 is a factor 100; 1,000; 10,000; and any number 10^x , where $x \geq 2$. To test for divisibility by 4 look at the 2-digit number in the tens and ones place and see if it is divisible by 4.

Eight is a factor of any number 10^x, where $x \geq 3$, therefore you must test the 3-digit number in the hundreds, tens, and ones place and see if it is divisible by 8. However, since 8 is a factor of 200; 400; 600; and 800, if the hundreds place is even, you need only test if the 2-digit number in the tens and ones place is divisible by 8.

When 100 is divided by 8, there is a remainder of 4. Every odd number multiple of 100 can be written as the sum of an even multiple of 100 plus 100 (900 = 800 + 100). Therefore, if the number in the hundreds place is odd, there will be a remainder of 4 when these 100s are divided by 8. To check for divisibility by 8, add 4 to the 2-digit number in the tens and ones place and see if that sum is divisible by 8.

Math Vocabulary and Symbols

Use and reinforcement of math vocabulary enables students to develop fluency. For instance, as soon as multiplication is introduced, teachers should begin using the words *product*, *multiple*, and *factor*. (Example: The product of 5 times 4 is 20. 20 is a multiple of 4. 5 is a factor of 20.)

When comparing numbers, the words such as *interval*, *less than*, *more than*, *at least,* and *at most* should be practiced.

Students ask, "Does less than 37 mean it includes 37? Does greater than 75 mean it excludes 75?" Both these descriptions exclude these numbers. What are the words that would include 37? (At most) What are the words that would include 75? (At least).

Another question often asked is about opened and closed intervals. "Does the description of the interval in symbols 29 < number < 63, include or exclude 29 and 63?" The symbol for including both end points would be 29 ≤ number ≤ 63. Students love learning symbols and codes!

Lexicon Activity Sheet

(Page 142)

Give each student a hard cardstock sheet with boxes for new math vocabulary words entitled, "My Math Lexicon Sheet." The sheet should be available for each math lesson. Teachers are amazed at how eager students are to add new words to their Lexicon Sheet and often suggest words for the sheet. Students love to watch the boxes fill up!

My Math Lexicon Sheet

Picturing Equivalent Fractions

Here are two methods of picturing equivalent fractions.

Method 1

$$\frac{2}{3} = \frac{?}{9}$$

Ask students to divide the following rectangle into thirds.

Ask them to shade in two of the thirds.

How can these be divided into ninths?

How many ninths fit into the 2/3s? Count them.

$$\frac{2}{3} = \frac{6}{9}$$

Method 2

This method needs a story. I have 9 candies.

My friend Sarah sees Sam with all this candy and asks where he got it. He tells her that I gave him the 6 candies.

Sarah comes to me to see if she can get some candy too. I tell her that I have another group of nine candies, and she can have 2 out of 3.

She thinks I am favoring Sam, so I tell her to divide the 9 candies into piles of three and then take 2 from each pile of three. I tell my friend Sam he can choose 6 of them. He chooses the ones he wants and thanks me.

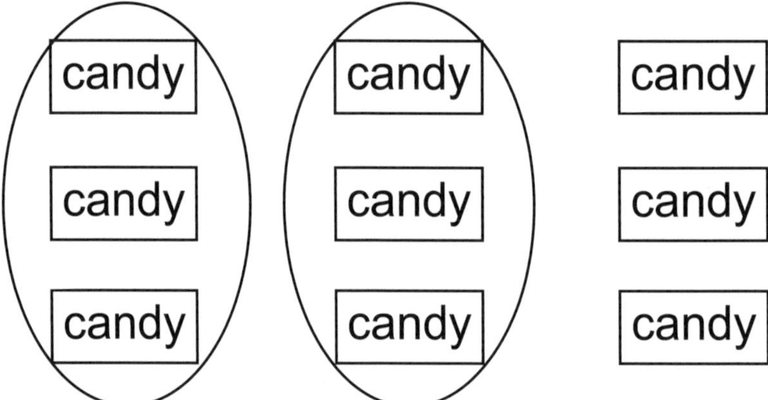

Sarah is delighted because she also got 6 candies. "Oh, I see," she says. "Taking 6 out of the 9 candies is the same as taking 2 out of every 3 candies!"

$$\frac{2}{3} = \frac{6}{9}$$

Exploring Proper Fractions, Improper Fractions, and Mixed Numbers

This activity encourages a discussion about why we express fractions in different forms. There is no right answer to the questions below. Each student must explain why she/he chose her/his answer.

The neighborhood pizza store accepts texts as orders to be delivered. Three people text an order for the same amount of pizza. Which of the texts below is easiest for you to figure out how much pizza is to be delivered to each of these customers? Assume each slice of pizza is 1/8 of a whole pie, and each whole pie is cut into eighths.

Customer #1	Customer #2	Customer #3
Please deliver 2 and 1/8 pizza pies.	Please deliver this amount of slices.	Please deliver $\frac{17}{8}$ slices of pizza.

Now, three people text you orders for the same amount of pizza, but they want every 4 slices in a different box. Which text is easiest for you to figure out how many boxes you need?

Customer #1	Customer #2	Customer #3
Please deliver 2 and 1/8 pizza pies.	Please deliver this amount of 1/8 slices.	Please deliver $\frac{17}{8}$ slices of pizza.

Next, three people text orders for cans of soda. For each slice of pizza, they want one can of soda. Which text is easiest for you to figure out how many cans of soda you need?

Customer #1	Customer #2	Customer #3
Please deliver 2 and 1/8 pizza pies.	Please deliver this amount of 1/8 slices.	Please deliver $\frac{17}{8}$ slices of pizza.

WHERE'S the MATH?
Math Concepts and Skills

Game	Number Sense	Operational Skills Practice	Place Value	Fractions	Decimals	Math Vocabulary and Symbols
1. Greater Than, Less Than	*	*	*	*	*	*
2. Stand Up and be Counted!	*	*				*
3. Clap Your Hands! Stomp Your Feet!	*	*				
4. Can You Make…?	*	*	*			
5. Math in a Circle	*	*	*	*	*	*
6. Fill the Grid!	*	*				
7. I Know My Place	*		*		*	
8. Top Ten With a Twist!	*	*				
9. Let's Sum Up: Odd or Even?	*	*				
10. Mulit-Math Bingo	*	*	*	*	*	*
11. Place Cards – You're Invited!	*	*	*			

12. Order Me!	*	*		*		
13. A or B or C? Where Should I Place the Number?	*	*	*		*	*
14. Primes, Composites, Perfect Squares, Factors, Multiples	*	*				*
15. Fraction Recipes	*	*		*		
16. Cube Structures	*	*		*		
17. Fraction/ Decimal Card Game	*	*		*	*	*
18. Clothesline Fractions and Decimals	*	*		*	*	
19. Make 1	*	*		*		
20. Teachable Moments	*	*	*	*		*

25. Who travels the longest distance? Who travels the shortest distance?

Tanya walks 4 feet every second for 60 seconds.

Kevin cycles 30 feet every second for 7 seconds.

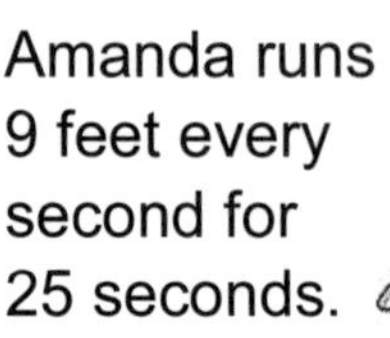

Amanda runs 9 feet every second for 25 seconds.

26. Joanne and Remy each build a wooden fence around their rectangular vegetable garden. Whose fence costs more?

Joanne's fence costs $7 per meter.

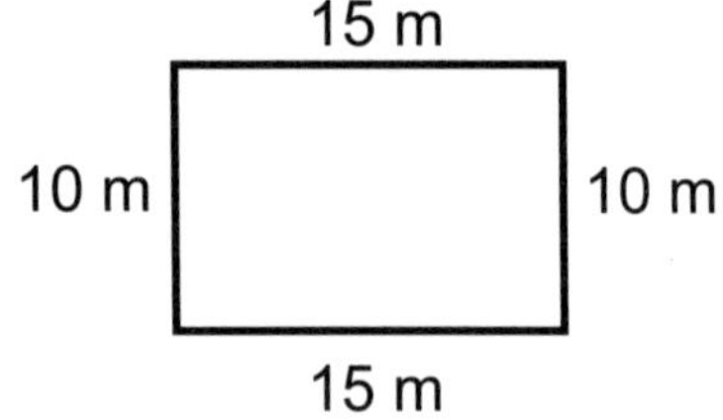

Remy's fence costs $5 per meter.

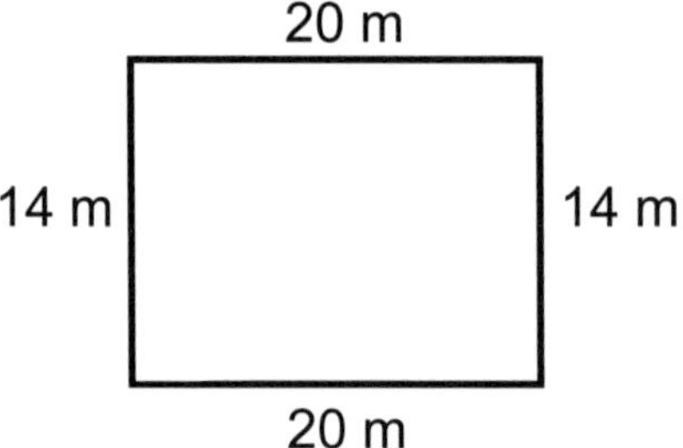

27. In the list below, each person's heart beats at a constant rate. Whose heart will have the most beats in 1 minute? Whose heart will have the fewest beats in 1 minute?

- Adam's heart beats 25 times in 20 seconds.
- Rachel's heart beats 160 times in 120 seconds.
- Brett's heart beats 18 times in 15 seconds.

37. Which is a longer amount of time?

a. 450 minutes or 7 hours

b. 1,000 seconds or 20 minutes

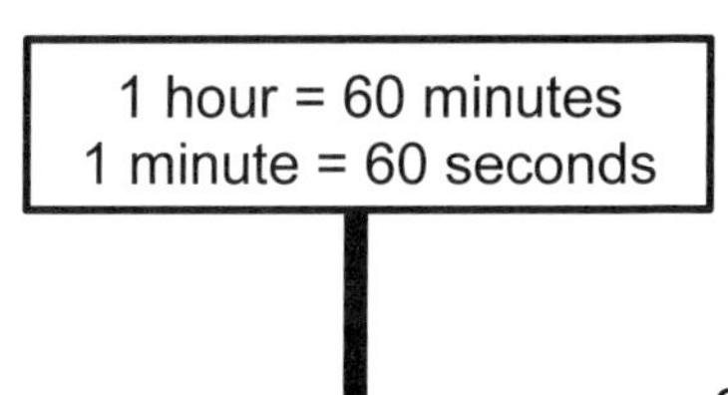

c. 190 minutes or $3\frac{1}{3}$ hours

d. 4,000 seconds or 1 hour

38. What is the price of a pencil? What is the price of a pen? What is the price of an eraser?

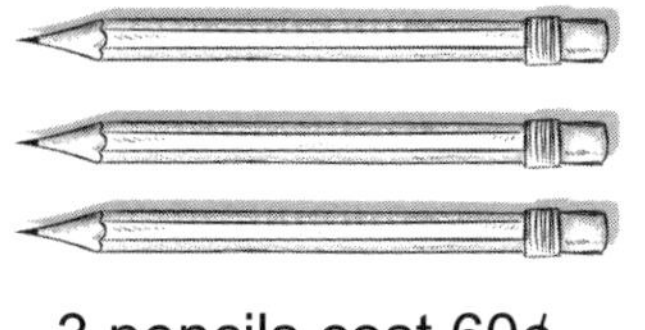

3 pencils cost 60¢

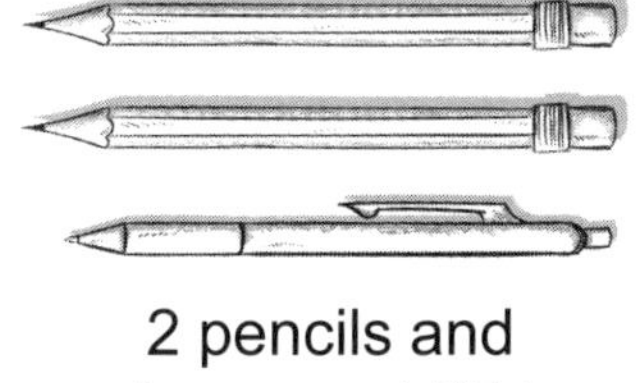
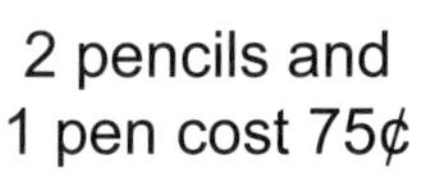

2 pencils and
1 pen cost 75¢

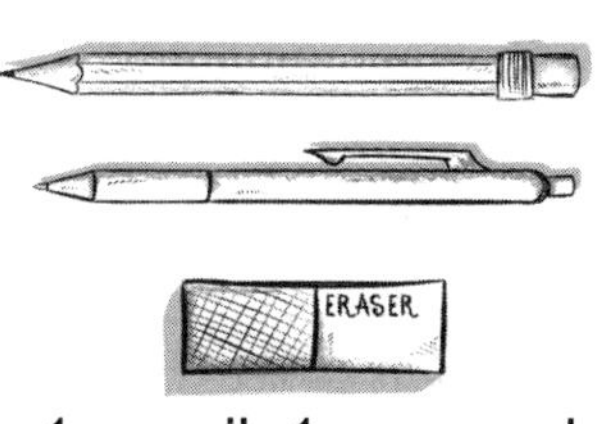

1 pencil, 1 pen, and
1 eraser cost $1.15

39. Which shaded region has the largest area? Which shaded region has the smallest area?

A

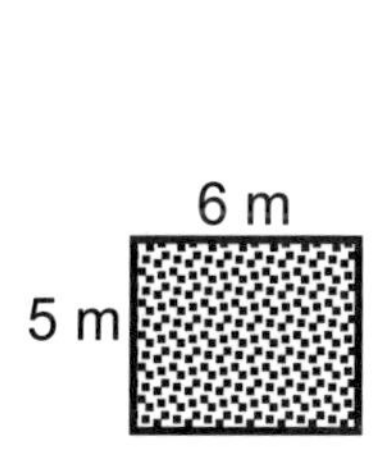

B

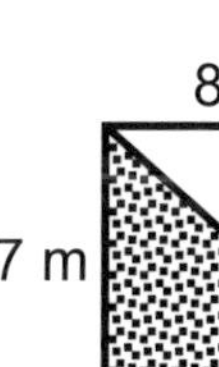
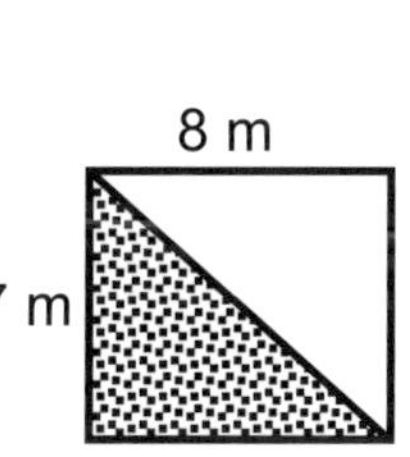

C

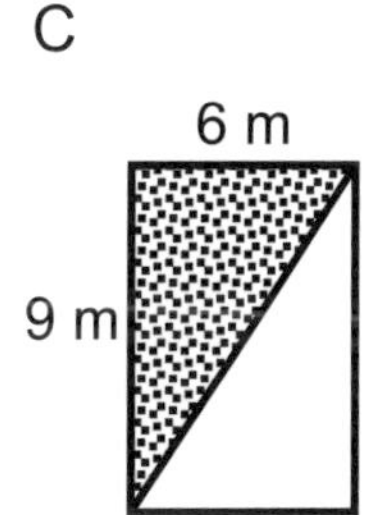

D

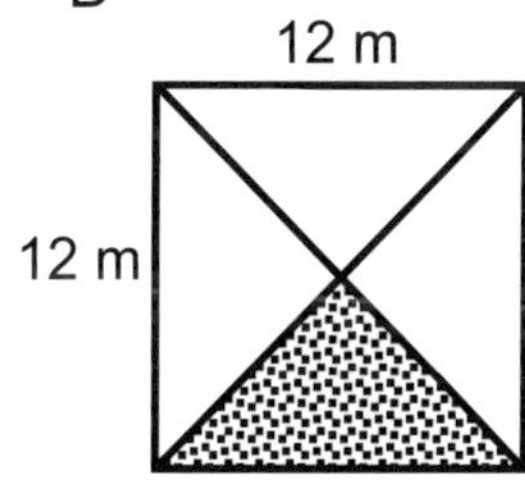

E

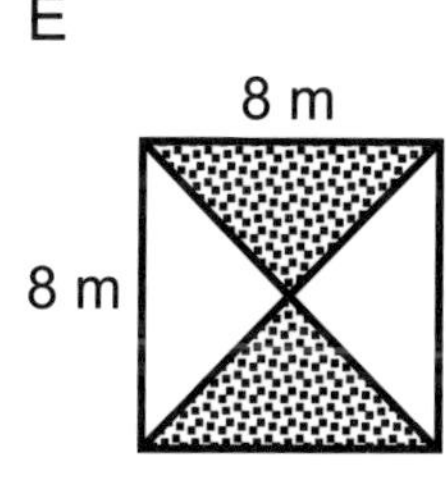

103. Whose car has more gas left after their trip?

Flora's car starts with 11 gallons of gas and she drives 150 miles.

Flora's car travels 30 miles for every gallon of gas.

Mason's car starts with 14 gallons of gas and he drives 175 miles.

Mason's car travels 25 miles for every gallon of gas.

104. Whose meal has more calories?

Jonah's meal
- 8 ounces of chicken
- 3 ounces of rice
- 6 ounces of beans

Camilla's meal
- 6 ounces of chicken
- 6 ounces of rice
- 5 ounces of beans

Nutrition Information
- 4 ounces of chicken has 200 calories
- 6 ounces of rice has 240 calories
- 2 ounces of beans has 60 calories

105. Whose jar holds more water when full?

Nora's jar is 2/3 full, but if she adds 6 more cups it will be completely full.

Robin's jar is 3/4 full, but if she adds 5 more cups it will be completely full.

Sample Activity From
Pattern Explorer Level 1

21. Pattern Predictor 5

The figures below are constructed from unit squares. Stage 2 has 4 unit squares: 3 shaded and 1 unshaded.

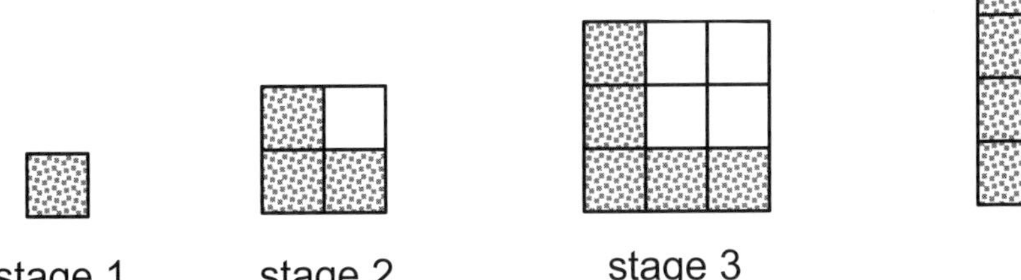

1. Complete the table to describe the pattern.

stage	1	2	3	4	5	6	7	8
# of unshaded unit squares	0	1						
# of shaded unit squares	1	3						
total # of unit squares	1	4						

2. How many unshaded unit squares are there at stage 11?

3. How many shaded unit squares are there at stage 14?

4. What is the total number of unit squares at stage 15?

5. At what stage are there 35 shaded unit squares?

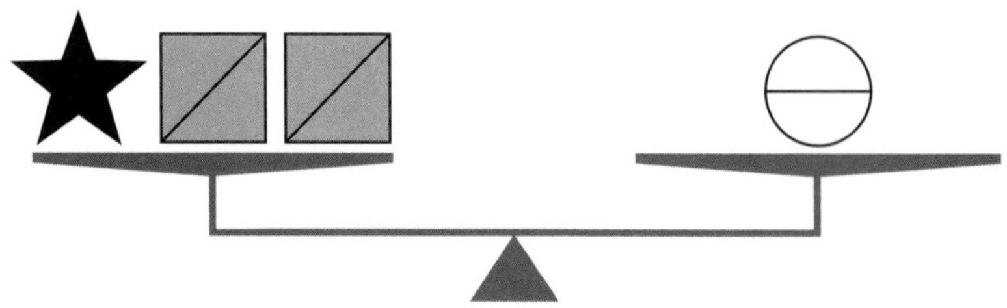

Circle the three answers below that will always be true.

a. d.

b. e.

c. f.